Ice Creams, Sorbets, Mousses & Parfaits

An extravaganza of delectable sweet and savoury dishes using
wholefood ingredients in tempting and unusual combinations.

Ice Creams, Sorbets, Mousses & Parfaits

The Delicious Natural Way

by

Jenny Allday

Illustrated by Paul Turner

BOOK CLUB ASSOCIATES
LONDON

This edition was published 1982 by
Book Club Associates
By arrangement with Thorsons Publishers Limited.

Photoset by Glebe Graphics, Wilby, Northamptonshire.
Printed in Great Britain by
The Thetford Press Limited, Thetford, Norfolk
and bound by Weatherby Woolnough,
Wellingborough, Northamptonshire.

Contents

Introduction

Why go to all the trouble of making your own ices when you can go out to a shop and buy them? In this book I try to tell you why I find it so worthwhile, and to show you, if you have never tried it yourself, what you are missing. Of course, the fact that you have picked up this book in the first place may mean that I am preaching to the converted, but if that is the case, I hope you will find new ideas to extend your repertoire.

First, consider the ingredients. The only way to be certain of what goes into an ice cream is to make it yourself. There are many regulations relating to ice cream, what goes into them and how they are made, but it is still legal to make ice cream without cream or butter, provided this is indicated on the label by a notice such as 'contains non-milk fat'. Apart from this, there is as yet no legal requirement to print the ingredients on the outside of the pack.

Ice cream in Great Britain (though things are now improving) has had rather a sad career over the past fifty years, from luxury to convenience to junk food. Ice cream was, once upon a time, an exotic treat for very special occasions. Later, the advent of commercial refrigeration at the beginning of the century made it possible for people to buy ice cream in shops, and it had to be made cheaply enough to be within the range of everyone's pocket. After the Second World War, when cream, eggs and sugar were difficult to come by, substitutes such as soya flour, vegetable oils and lactose came into use; synthetic flavourings and colourings, and highly refined emulsifiers and stabilizers were developed in an attempt to give them the taste and texture of an old-fashioned ice cream.

The trend is now towards more natural ingredients (though the irony of messages such as; 'ice cream with *real* cream' and: 'with *real* strawberries' still hits me when I see them on the label); nevertheless, the additives are still with us.

If you make your own ice cream, you can be sure that your ingredients are not only natural but, as far as possible, unrefined. Also the range of commercial ice cream can never equal the range and variety you can produce yourself.

For many years after the war we were restricted to no more than six flavours of ice cream, and most of those synthetic. Now we can buy Italian ice cream, and commercial producers can buy a wide range of Italian flavours, actually made with fruit and nuts. American ice creams are also making an appearance in our High Streets, in twenty or thirty different flavours. However, as you will see from this book, at home your range is practically limitless – from savoury starters to sophisticated dinner party creations; from simple foods for children and treats to tempt an invalid, to delectable fattening puddings which will send you rushing to the bathroom scales.

Furthermore, you can control the sweetness and richness of your mixtures. To my taste, all the commercial ice creams are too sweet. At home, it is possible to make ice cream which is less sweet, and which will be enjoyed even by people who think they do not like ice cream.

It may be objected that making ice cream involves a lot of work. Certainly it is no good thinking you are going to throw together an ice cream an hour before your guests are due for a dinner party. You really need to start well in advance. Ideally, for special occasions, make up the mixture the evening before and chill it in the refrigerator overnight. Set aside a day when you know you are going to be at home for three or four hours, because your ice cream will need attention from time to time to help along the freezing process, and it should mature for an hour or two after it is frozen and before you serve it. But the making of the basic mix will take you no more than ten minutes, and the total time you spend on it will be no more than thirty to forty-five minutes.

Lastly, you will say it is fattening. Obviously, a food of which two of the main ingredients are sugar and cream is bound to be fattening if you make it your staple diet; but you will find a section on alternatives to cream, and also alternatives to sugar, and the advantage of making your own ice cream is that you can control the quantities of cream and sugar that go into it.

1. Basic Knowledge

Once you have grasped the basic principles of ice cream making, I hope you will experiment for yourself. To achieve an ice cream which is smooth, creamy, and not too hard, it is helpful to know one or two facts.

Ingredients:
If you freeze a pint of cream it will be rock solid and very difficult to serve. The *sugar* you add acts not only as a sweetener: it also controls how soft your ice cream will be. Too much sugar, and it will not freeze, too little and it will freeze too hard.

Salt added to the recipe will also slow down freezing. Be careful, though. A little salt will enhance the flavour, too much will give it an unpleasant taste. Where egg whites are used in the recipe, the salt is best added to them as you whisk them.

Alcohol also stops the mix freezing. Ice creams incorporating wine or spirits will never freeze as hard as those without them. Ice creams with alcohol have the advantage that they can be eaten straight from the freezer without waiting for them to soften, but beware; if you are over-lavish you will have problems in getting them to freeze at all.

Egg whites. How light or solid you like your ice cream is obviously a matter of personal taste, but the more air you whip in, the lighter it will be. In commercial ice cream this is referred to as the 'overrun', and can be as much as 100 per cent. You can never achieve this with a home-made ice cream, and probably would not want to, but whipped cream and whisked egg white will both help to incorporate air. If an ice cream is firmer than you like, add another whisked egg white next time.

To produce a thicker, creamier mixture which will hold the air you beat in, and which will not separate during freezing, you may want to use a stabilizer. The egg yolk, which is an ingredient in most of the recipes for ice cream, is important for this. Both agar agar and arrowroot, used according to directions, are useful. Do not overdo them though, or your ice cream will have a gluey texture.

Equipment:

To achieve a smooth, velvety ice cream, frequent beating is necessary to break up the little granules of fat and also to stop ice crystals forming in the mixture. In America, ice cream churns, electrically operated, are readily available for this. In Great Britain they are hard to come by and expensive. They undoubtedly produce a smooth and velvety ice cream, but unless you are going to make ice cream in great quantities, they are hardly worth the expense. A churn is not necessary for any of the recipes in this book, but with the exception of iced mousses, which can be left to freeze undisturbed, you will have to remember to stir the mixture from time to time as it freezes.

Note: It is possible to buy small domestic ice cream makers with electrically rotating paddles which you put in your refrigerator or freezer. I have tried one of these, but it has found its way to the attic, with other discarded equipment. There was no room for it in the freezing compartment of my refrigerator, and clearing a level space for it in the freezer also proved a problem.

This brings us to the equipment you will find useful, most of it standard equipment which you probably already have.

Although it is possible to manage by hand, *an electric blender* will dramatically cut the time it takes to make fruit *purées*, beat sorbets, chop nuts, etc.

An *electric mixer* is also well worth investing in, preferably one with a dough hook.

As for the smaller items of equipment, *kitchen scales* are a must. Always weigh your ingredients the first time you try a recipe. The amount of sugar you put in is particularly critical.

You will also need a *measuring jug*, marked with pints and fluid ounces.

A *sugar thermometer* is useful for making syrups, and will save a lot of hovering and worrying when you are making toffee, fudge or praline with raw cane sugar. It is difficult to judge the temperature by eye, as can be done with white sugar.

The easiest way to make custard is in a *double boiler*, but you can use a bowl on top of a saucepan instead. A metal bowl is best as you can move it from cooker to freezer without fear of it cracking.

You will also need a *spatula*, a *wooden spoon* and a *nylon sieve* for making fruit *purées*.

The Time Factor

The time that the ice cream will take from first chilling in the refrigerator until it is frozen solid is hard to gauge. It will depend on the temperature of your equipment, the weather, the season, the temperature in your kitchen, the quantity of the ice cream and the size and shape of the container.

Having said all that, put the mixture to chill in the refrigerator for two to three hours before freezing, then transfer it to the freezer. After three to four hours in the freezer, during which you have scraped the sides to the middle of the bowl once or twice so that it freezes evenly, it should be ready for the final beating. Pack, and allow two more hours for it to freeze solid, then a further two hours for it to mature.

Note: Water ices freeze more quickly. You need allow only two to three hours in the freezer before beating.

Freezing

Ice creams, to be at their best, should be frozen quickly. The process is speeded up if you can remember the following points.

1. Always chill your equipment – bowls, whisks, spatulas – in the refrigerator before use.
2. To cool a mixture quickly, plunge the bowl with its contents into a bowl of cold water or ice cubes.
3. Chill your mixture for at least an hour in the refrigerator before freezing.
4. If making ice cream in the refrigerator, turn the setting of the freezing compartment to coldest at least half an hour before you use it. If you are using a freezer, turn the setting to 'Quick Freeze'.
5. A metal container will freeze your mixture fastest. (*Note:* for acid fruit, avoid all metals except stainless steel, or the acid will react with the metal.)
6. Ice cream will freeze faster spread out in a shallow container.
7. If using the freezer, if possible leave one side of the container in contact with the sides or bottom of the freezer. Always leave space for air to circulate round the container.

Storing

1. Always use a lidded container to store your ice cream. Plastic tubs are ideal, and if they are square or rectangular you will find they save space in the freezer, and are easier to stack. Don't forget to label them and put the date on.

2. Store ice creams in containers of the right size, so that they can be eaten at one sitting. Once the air gets to ice cream it develops ice crystals which spoil the texture.

If you unavoidably have a half-full container in the freezer, put greaseproof paper or cling film over the ice cream in the container to exclude the air.

3. Ice cream will keep for up to three months in the freezer, provided the temperature is constant. After that it may darken in colour and shrink away from the edges. It will be quite safe to eat, but it will not look as appetizing.

4. If the nightmare happens and you have a freezer breakdown, ice cream that has melted separates out and will have to be thrown away. If it has softened but not melted, you can refreeze it without harm to health, but you may find that the texture has deteriorated. It may have ice crystals and it will be more solid in texture.

Serving

If you are making your ice to eat the same day, it is much improved if left in the freezer for a couple of hours after it has completely frozen, to ripen.

With the exception of those containing alcohol, home-made ices need to be softened when you take them out of the freezer, before serving. The length of time necessary varies according to the ice cream recipe and the size and depth of the container. As a rough guide, a small container (approx. 1 pint) should be put in the refrigerator for 30-45 minutes. A four-pint container will take up to two hours. In an emergency, the ice cream can be softened at room temperature but you will find that the outside edges melt before the middle is softened.

To serve a moulded ice cream, unmould immediately you take it from the freezer. Dip the mould in warm water for a few seconds. Dry it, ease the edges with a knife and turn out. Then leave to soften in the refrigerator.

Note: Water ices thaw more quickly than ice cream, so allow a little less time.

Final Hints to the Cook

1. When making syrup, remember that raw cane sugar, molasses and honey will always boil up. Choose a large saucepan and watch it carefully.

2. Do not overbeat the cream. This will give the ice cream an over-firm, buttery texture.

3. Remember that food tastes less when cold, so wait until the mixture is cold before you taste it, and always over-flavour and over-sweeten, so that it tastes right once it is frozen.

4. When you are experimenting, remember the fruits which discolour most easily when you *purée* them raw. Prevent this by sprinkling with lemon juice such fruits as apples, bananas, grapes, greengages, pears, plums.

5. Things to do with your left over egg yolks and whites:

Yolks: use in iced mousse without whites (see basic recipe); use in mayonnaise; or freeze them, adding 1 teaspoonful sea salt or raw cane sugar to seven yolks.

Whites: use in iced *soufflés* (see basic recipe); meringues (see the section on Stores); macaroons; or freeze them in individual cubes in an ice tray for use later.

There are several methods of making cream ices. A section on each method follows, starting with the basic recipe. Having tried all the methods and decided which you prefer for texture and taste, the flavourings are largely interchangeable.

The recommended sugar for most of the recipes is light muscovado, but this can be varied according to taste, bearing in mind that the darker sugars will overwhelm the more delicate flavourings.

2. Custard Base Ice Creams

Ice cream made with a custard base is the least rich, having the least cream, and it is also the most economical. Many of the ice creams in the book can be adapted to this method, but it is risky to use it for ice cream with fruit, particularly acid fruit, which may curdle the custard.

An ice made entirely with milk will end up with a crunchy rather than a creamy texture, because of its lower fat content. However, if you wish to cut down on the cream, add a little arrowroot to the milk and boil it until it thickens, before pouring it on the egg yolks (1 teaspoonful mixed to a paste with a little cold milk will be enough to thicken ¾ pint of milk. If you are heavy-handed with the arrowroot, you will end up with a gluey texture).

Basic recipe:

2 eggs
2 egg yolks
3 oz (75g) raw cane sugar
1 pt (550ml) milk
¼ pt (140ml) whipping cream

Break the eggs and egg yolks into a bowl, add the sugar and beat until thick and creamy. Heat the milk until it is just about to boil and pour over the egg mixture in a steady stream, whisking all the time. Pour the mixture back into the saucepan and cook over a low heat, stirring constantly, until the custard begins to thicken and coat the back of the spoon, but do not let it boil, or it will curdle. (*Note:* to lessen the risk of curdling, this may be done either in a double boiler, or in a bowl over a saucepan of hot water.)

Remove the custard from the heat and place the saucepan or bowl in a bowl of cold water, or better still, a bowl of ice cubes, to hasten the cooling process.

Meanwhile whip the cream until firm, and then fold it into the cooled custard mixture, chill and freeze.

As it hardens, push the sides of the mixture to the middle. When nearly set, beat it, then pack and freeze.

This is the basic recipe. When you add the flavouring of your choice remember to over-flavour and over-sweeten, if anything, as the freezing process diminishes the taste. Quantities will be enough for six to eight people unless otherwise stated.

VANILLA ICE CREAM

The easiest way of dealing with vanilla is to keep two vanilla pods in a screw-top jar full of light raw cane sugar. This way you will always have vanilla-flavoured sugar. The alternative is to simmer the pods with the cream, as indicated in the following recipe.

2 eggs
2 egg yolks
3 oz (75g) raw cane sugar
1 pt (550ml) milk
1 vanilla pod
¼ pt (140ml) double cream, lightly whipped

First, in a small saucepan scald the milk with the vanilla pod (bring to just below boiling point) then cover, remove from heat and leave to infuse for twenty minutes. Break the whole eggs into a bowl, add the egg yolks and sugar and whisk to mix well. Strain the milk onto the eggs and sugar, stirring constantly. Now proceed as for the basic custard recipe.

CHESTNUT ICE CREAM

2 eggs
2 egg yolks
3 oz (75g) light muscovado sugar
1 pt (550ml) milk
¼ pt (140ml) double cream
1 vanilla pod
For the chestnut purée:
1 10 oz (275g) tin unsweetened chestnut purée (or you may prefer
to purée your own)
1 lb (450g) light muscovado sugar
¼ pt (140ml) water

Make a heavy syrup by dissolving the muscovado sugar in the water;
bring to the boil and boil fast for three minutes. Cool and beat into the
chestnut *purée*. Follow the recipe for vanilla ice cream, but when you
get to the packing stage, pack in alternate layers of ice cream and
chestnut *purée*, finishing with ice cream.

Variation: Mix half the sweetened chestnut *purée* into the ice cream just
before you add the whipped cream. Reserve the other half, and spoon a
dollop onto each helping when you serve it.

COCONUT COOKIE ICE

½ pt (275ml) milk
4 eggs
1 egg white
2 oz (50g) light muscovado sugar
½ pt (275ml) cream
5 oz (150g) creamed coconut
1 oz (25g) freshly grated or desiccated coconut
3 oz (75g) coarsely crushed coconut cookies (see the section on
Stores)

Separate the eggs. Beat the egg yolks with the sugar in a medium-sized
mixing bowl. Bring the milk to boiling point and pour it over the egg
yolks, whisking all the time. Return to the saucepan and stir over a low

heat until the mixture thickens and coats the back of the spoon. Remove from the heat. Melt the creamed coconut and add to the mixture. If you are using desiccated coconut, add this now. Set aside to cool. Whip the cream and fold this into the mixture. Whip the egg whites and fold in. Chill and freeze. Just before packing add the crushed coconut cookies (large enough pieces to be crunchy) and the fresh coconut if used.

Note: The egg whites in this recipe are important, as creamed coconut sets rock hard, and they help to lighten the ice cream.

COFFEE ICE CREAM

2 eggs
2 egg yolks
3 oz (75g) light muscovado sugar
1 pt (550ml) milk
2 oz (50g) coffee beans
¼ pt (140ml) double cream, lightly whipped

In a small saucepan, scald the milk with the coffee beans and infuse over a very low heat for 45 minutes. The milk should not boil. Meanwhile, break the whole eggs into a bowl, add the egg yolks and the sugar and whisk to mix well. Strain the milk onto the eggs and sugar, stirring all the time, and discard the coffee beans. Now proceed as for the basic custard recipe.

Variation: Add ½ oz chopped walnuts mixed with 1 tablespoonful maple syrup when you add the whipped cream.

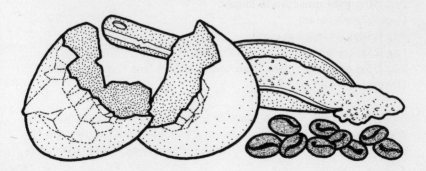

CHOCOLATE ICE CREAM

4 egg yolks
2 oz (50g) raw cane sugar
½ pt (275 ml) cream
½ pt (275 ml) milk
6 oz (175g) plain chocolate

Beat the egg yolks with the sugar in a medium-sized mixing bowl. Bring the milk nearly to the boil and pour over the egg yolks, stirring all the time. Set aside. Break the chocolate into a bowl and pour boiling water over it to melt. Now return the egg yolks, sugar and milk to the saucepan over a low heat and stir all the time until it coats the back of the spoon. Take it off the heat. Pour the water carefully off the chocolate, and add the chocolate to the egg mixture. Mix well and set aside to cool. Whip the cream and fold into the mixture, chill and freeze.

Variations:
1. Use a 9 oz carob bar instead of plain chocolate.
2. Add chopped coffee-flavoured fudge or chopped toasted hazelnuts to the ice cream just before you fold in the cream.
3. Add a spoonful of strong coffee to the chocolate and, if you are celebrating, a spoonful of brandy or rum. Remember that if you are too lavish with the brandy or rum, you may have difficulty in freezing the mixture.

CHOCOLATE TRUFFLE ICE CREAM

½ pt (275 ml) milk
4 egg yolks
2 oz (50g) raw cane sugar
½ pt (275 ml) cream
3 oz (75g) plain chocolate
3 oz (75g) ground hazelnuts

Beat the egg yolks with the sugar in a medium-sized mixing bowl until thick. Scald the milk and pour over the egg yolks, stirring all the time. Set aside while you break the chocolate into a bowl and pour boiling water over it to melt. Now return the egg yolks, sugar and milk to the saucepan and stir over a low heat until it coats the back of the spoon. Remove from the heat and continue stirring for a few moments. Pour the water carefully off the chocolate and beat the chocolate into the egg mixture. Add the ground hazelnuts. Set aside to cool. Whip the cream and fold into the mixture. Chill and freeze.

CINNAMON ICE CREAM

¾ pt (425 ml) milk
3 egg yolks
¼ pt (140 ml) water
4 oz (100 g) honey
½ teaspoonful arrowroot
1 vanilla pod
3 cinnamon sticks
1 teaspoonful ground cinnamon
pinch of sea salt
¼ pt (140 ml) whipped cream

Put the honey, water, cinnamon sticks and vanilla pod into a saucepan and cook for ten minutes, until syrupy. Discard the cinnamon sticks and vanilla pod and allow to cool. Beat the egg yolks until pale and creamy. Mix the arrowroot with 2 tablespoonsful of water. Bring the milk to the boil with the arrowroot, stirring to dissolve. Keep at boiling point for a few seconds, then pour over the beaten egg yolks. Return to the saucepan and cook until thickened, but do not let it boil. Remove from the heat and allow to cool, stirring from time to time. Add the cinnamon syrup, more spices if liked, and a pinch of salt. Add the whipped cream and freeze.

Note: This recipe uses arrowroot, which helps to give a creamier texture and also to give more volume when you beat the mixture.

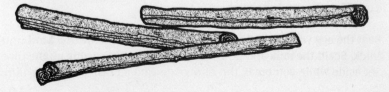

HAZELNUT ICE CREAM

2 eggs
2 egg yolks
3 oz (75 g) light muscovado sugar
1 pt (550 ml) milk
¼ pt (140 ml) whipping cream
3 oz (75 g) hazelnut and light muscovado mixture (see section on Stores)

Make up the ice cream according to the basic recipe. Stir in the hazelnut and sugar mixture just before you fold in the whipped cream.

TOFFEE ICE CREAM

2 eggs
2 egg yolks
2 oz (50 g) raw cane sugar
1 pt (550 ml) milk
¼ pt (140 ml) whipping cream
For the caramel:
4 oz (100 g) raw cane sugar
6-7 fl oz (approx. 180 ml) water
squeeze lemon juice (optional)

To make the caramel, dissolve the sugar with 4 fl oz water in a thick bottomed saucepan over a low heat, stirring from time to time. When it is melted, boil fast* (280°F on your sugar thermometer) until it turns to a rich syrup. Now take it from the heat and add the remaining 3 fl oz water by degrees, stirring as you do so. It is liable to splutter and splash at this stage, so go carefully. Finally add a squeeze of lemon juice if liked. When cool, it is ready for use or storage in a screw-top jar. It should, when cold, form a thick syrup.

To make toffee ice cream, add ¼ pint caramel to the basic ice cream mix just before you fold in the whipped cream.

Note: Because of the extra sugar, this will be a fairly soft ice cream, so you will not need to soften it in the refrigerator for as long as most ice cream before you serve it.

For the same reason, do not add more caramel than the recipe says, or you will have trouble in freezing the mixture.

•Remember that raw cane sugar will boil up and must be watched and stirred at this stage.

Variation: **BURNT ORANGE ICE CREAM**
For a delicious variation on toffee ice cream, when you make your caramel, instead of adding 3 fl oz of water to the syrup, add 3 fl oz of orange juice, and for added flavour, leave the thinly peeled rind of the orange in the caramel while it cools. Add ¼ pint of this to the ice cream recipe. Check the flavour. Fold in the whipped cream and freeze.

To serve: Sprinkle with grated zest of orange.

3. Iced Mousses and Parfaits

The method for this ice cream is to make a rich custard and add whipped cream. Sometimes the yolks of eggs alone are used, and sometimes the stiffly beaten whites are added after the whipped cream. (This makes a lighter ice cream which is also slightly quicker to soften before serving.) If you are going to eat it the same day, remember it will be even better if, once frozen, you leave it in the freezer for at least half an hour before removing it to soften.

Quantities in recipes for fruit mousses and parfaits are for eight to ten people.

4 egg yolks
4 oz (100g) raw cane sugar
¾ pt (425 ml) cream
¼ pt (140 ml) water
flavouring

Method 1
Beat the egg yolks until thick and creamy. Boil the sugar and water together in a small pan for five minutes, or until the syrup reaches 220°-230°F on your sugar thermometer. Pour the syrup over the egg yolks in a steady stream, beating all the time, and continue to beat until cool. Whip the cream and fold into the egg mixture. Chill and freeze. When it is beginning to set, remove from the freezer, beat, and return to the freezer.

For this method, it is obviously a great advantage to have an electric beater. If it has a dough hook, this is the ideal tool for the final beating.

Method 2
First scald half the cream (bring to the boil) and pour it on to the beaten egg yolks, whisking all the time. Omit the water. Mix in the sugar and put the bowl over a saucepan of boiling water, stirring until it thickens to a custard. Set aside to cool. Whip the other half of the cream and fold it into the custard. Chill and freeze. Stir the sides into the middle as it begins to harden.

When the mixture is nearly set, remove it from the freezer and beat it before packing it into the container in which you wish to store it.

Note:
1. All the recipes in this section involve the addition of either fruit *purée* or flavouring such as fudge, which must be beaten in just before you pack the ice cream. If, however, you wish to use the basic recipe for a plain ice cream such as vanilla or coffee you can omit the final beating.
2. Although this mixture is referred to as a mousse, do not be tempted to thaw it out and serve it as an unfrozen mousse, it will separate.
3. Always remember to fold the cream in carefully. Any that is not thoroughly mixed in will be present in the finished ice cream as small leathery lumps, and so spoil the texture.

PARFAITS
The mixture and method for an iced mousse is also used for parfaits. The term 'parfait' refers to the way in which the iced mousse is served. It is generally made in a mould and served with sweetened whipped cream or fruit or a sauce.

You will find suggestions at the end of this section on how to serve them as parfaits, but it also provides an opportunity for you to branch out. Invent your own combinations of flavours and use different shapes of mould, be it ring moulds, jelly moulds or even a plain metal bowl, and use different garnishes to produce an impressive ice cream for special occasions.

Note: Unmoulding an ice cream is not nearly as unnerving as it sounds, especially if you use a metal mould. Before serving, remove the mould from the freezer and dip it into a bowl of warm water for a few seconds. Take it out, dry it, and turn out the ice cream onto a cold plate. You may need to slip a knife round the rim to loosen it first. Put it into the refrigerator to soften. The time this takes will vary according to the type of mixture and size of mould, but allow at least half an hour. If it looks as though it is getting too soft, return it to the freezer. Quantities for fruit mousses are for eight to ten people.

ICED APPLE MOUSSE

1½ lb (675g) cooking apples
a good strip of lemon rind
8 oz (225g) light muscovado sugar
4 egg yolks
¼ pt (140 ml) water
¾ pt (425 ml) whipping cream

Peel, core and chop the apples and stew with enough water to cover the bottom of the pan, 4 oz of the sugar and the strip of lemon rind. Remove the lemon rind and mash apples to a pulp, or put through a blender. Beat the egg yolks until thick and creamy. Boil the remaining 4 oz sugar with the water to 220°F on your sugar thermometer. Pour onto the egg yolks, beating all the time. Continue beating until the mixture is cool. Fold in the apple pulp, and lastly the stiffly whipped cream. Chill and freeze.

Variations:
1. Add ½ teaspoonful of cinnamon or two cloves to the apples when you stew them.
2. At the final beating, fold in 3 oz roughly crumbled hazelnut meringue, pack and freeze.
3. Scatter with toasted sunflower seeds before serving.

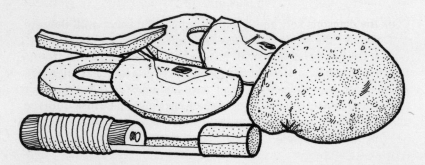

ICED CHERRY MOUSSE

1 1/4 lb (550g) cherries, preferably morello
6 oz (175g) honey
4 egg yolks
4 oz (100g) raw cane sugar
1/4 pt (140ml) water
3/4 pt (425ml) cream

Stone the cherries. Put 3/4 lb to stew with 2 tablespoonsful of water to extract the juice. Liquidize to a *purée*. Reserve the remaining 1/2 lb and soak in a little mild honey. (These are to be folded in just before packing. You must soak them in some sort of syrup, or they will be like little bullets in the finished ice cream.)

Make up the ice cream according to the basic recipe. Add the cherry *purée* just before you add the whipped cream. When you pack the ice cream, fold in the whole cherries.

ICED DAMSON MOUSSE

For the purée:
4 oz (100g) raw cane sugar
1 1/4 lb (550g) damsons
2 tablespoonsful water

4 oz (100g) raw cane sugar
1/4 pt (140ml) water
4 egg yolks
3/4 pt (425ml) cream

Cook the damsons very gently with the sugar and water until they are soft. Remove the stones and *purée* the fruit. Set aside to cool.

Beat the egg yolks in a small mixing bowl until yellow and frothy. Dissolve the sugar and water in a small pan over a low heat, then boil steadily until it reaches the thread stage and registers 220°F on your sugar thermometer. Pour onto the beaten egg yolks and whisk until the mixture is thick. Fold in the damson *purée*. Allow to cool.

Whip the cream, fold it into the damson mixture, chill and freeze.

ICED GREENGAGE MOUSSE

Greengages are difficult to handle because they discolour very easily once the skins are broken and they come into contact with air. If you want the taste of fresh uncooked greengages, you will have to resign yourself to a brown *purée*, or add colouring. The following recipe is for a very lightly cooked *purée*, which will be a rich golden colour.

For the purée:
1 lb (450g) greengages
½ pt (275ml) apple juice
6 tablespoonsful lemon juice

4 egg yolks
2 oz (50g) raw cane sugar
6 fl oz (165ml) apple juice
¾ pt (425ml) cream

For the *purée*, halve and stone the greengages, sprinkle quickly with lemon juice and drop into the apple juice. Simmer gently for seven minutes then mash with a fork to make a rough *purée*, or put through a sieve or a blender. Set aside to cool.

Following the method for the basic recipe, beat the egg yolks until pale and creamy. Melt the sugar in the apple juice, stirring to dissolve, and bring to the boil. Pour over the egg yolks in a steady stream, beating all the time, and continue beating until cool. Stir in the greengage *purée*. Whip the cream and fold into the mixture, chill and freeze.

ICED LOGANBERRY MOUSSE

This is best made with raw loganberries, which will produce an ice cream with a marvellous colour and a delicious taste.

For the purée:
1½ lb (675g) loganberries
2½ fl oz (70ml) red grape juice
4 oz (100g) raw cane sugar

4 egg yolks
4 oz (100g) raw cane sugar

¼pt (140ml) water
¼pt (140ml) whipping cream

Melt the sugar with the grape juice, blend with the loganberries and *purée* with a sieve or a blender. Set aside to cool.

Make up the mousse according to the basic recipe for this section and fold in the loganberry *purée* just before you add the whipped cream. Chill and freeze.

ICED PRUNE MOUSSE

For the purée:
1 lb (450g) prunes
1 pt (550ml) red wine
1 teaspoonful cinnamon
zest of 2 lemons
juice of 1 lemon

3 egg yolks
¾pt (425ml) whipping cream
6 oz (175g) light muscovado sugar
scant ¼pt (140ml) water
6 tablespoonsful rum − optional
1 oz (25g) chopped almonds or walnuts

Soak the prunes overnight in the red wine, then simmer them in the wine with the lemon zest, juice and cinnamon over a low heat with the lid on until they are tender. Allow to cool, then stone the prunes carefully and sieve or liquidize them.

Follow the basic recipe for this section, adding the prune *purée* to the egg yolk and syrup mixture just before the whipped cream. Just before packing, fold in the chopped nuts.

Note: You will have one peeled lemon left over from this recipe. If you have no immediate use for it, squeeze it, freeze the juice into ice cubes and store it in the freezer. I find these lemon juice cubes very useful for all sorts of things.

SPICED PLUM MOUSSE

For the purée:
1½ lb (675g) plums
1½ teaspoonsful cinnamon
1½ teaspoonsful nutmeg
1 clove or pinch of ground cloves
3 oz (75g) raw cane sugar
3 strips lemon peel
squeeze of lemon juice
3 tablespoonsful water

4 egg yolks
4 oz (100g) raw cane sugar
¼ pt (140ml) water
¾ pt (425ml) cream

Simmer the stoned plums with the sugar, spices, lemon peel and the water until soft. Set aside to cool. Remove the lemon peel and *purée* the spiced plum mixture. Check for taste and remember that spices, when frozen, diminish in flavour, so be generous.

Make up the ice cream according to the basic recipe, and just before adding the whipped cream fold in the plum *purée*.

Note: This *purée* is a delicious sauce to pour hot over other ices such as Maple Syrup, Brown Bread or Hazelnut, so it is worth making more than you need and storing it in the freezer. In this case, before serving, re-heat and thicken slightly with 1 level teaspoonful of arrowroot, previously soaked in 2 tablespoonsful of cold water. Bring to the boil, boil for a few seconds, then it is ready.

ICED STRAWBERRY MOUSSE

For the purée:
1½ lb (675g) fresh strawberries, puréed
¼ pt (140ml) red grape juice
2 tablespoonsful honey
juice of 1 lemon

4 egg yolks

4 oz (100g) raw cane sugar
¼ pt (140ml) water
¾ pt (425ml) cream

Melt the honey in the red grape juice with the lemon juice and add this mixture to the strawberry pulp. Taste and see if you need more lemon juice.

Now make the ice cream according to the basic recipe for this section. Just before folding in the cream, fold in the strawberry *purée*. Pack and freeze.

VICTORIA PLUM MOUSSE

For the purée:
1½ lb (675g) Victoria plums
3 oz (75g) honey
¼ pt (140ml) sweet cider
squeeze of lemon juice
1 teaspoonful arrowroot

4 egg yolks
4 oz (100g) honey
¼ pt (140ml) water
¾ pt (425ml) cream

Any good dessert plums, picked at their ripest and juiciest, will be suitable for this ice. It is possible to stone Victorias before putting them in the syrup. Other varieties may have to be stoned after stewing. Heat the honey, cider and lemon juice in a saucepan. Stone the plums and drop them immediately into the syrup so that they do not lose their colour. Mix the arrowroot with 2 tablespoonsful of cold water.

Bring the plums to the boil and simmer for three or four minutes. Add the arrowroot and stir to dissolve, then remove from the heat, cool and *purée*. The skins will give this *purée* a lovely colour.

Make the ice cream according to the basic recipe, and just before adding the whipped cream, fold in the plum *purée*. Serve sprinkled with pecan nuts.

ICED MOUSSE WITH EGG WHITES

Basic recipe:
6 egg yolks
7 egg whites
pinch of sea salt
4 oz (100g) light muscovado sugar
¼ pt (140ml) water
¾ pt (425ml) whipping cream

Separate the eggs and then proceed as for the previous recipe. After folding in the whipped cream, whisk the egg whites with a good pinch of salt until firm, and fold them into the mixture. Chill and freeze. When it is beginning to set, remove from the freezer and turn the hardening sides into the middle.

ICED ALMANDINE MOUSSE

6 egg yolks
7 egg whites
pinch of sea salt
4 oz (100g) raw cane sugar
¼ pt (140ml) water
¾ pt (425ml) whipping cream
2 oz (50g) ground almonds
1 teaspoonful rose-water – optional
¾ oz (75g) toasted flaked almonds

Beat the egg yolks until pale and creamy. Boil the sugar and water to the thread stage (220°F on the sugar thermometer). Pour the syrup over the egg yolks, whisking continuously, and continue whisking until cool. Add the rose-water (if you can get it) and the ground almonds. Allow to cool. Whip the cream and fold in. Whisk the egg whites with the salt until stiff. Fold this into the other mixture. Chill and freeze.

Just before packing, fold in the toasted flaked almonds. To serve, scatter a few flaked almonds on top. Serve on its own, or with a raspberry or apricot *purée*.

ICED BANANA AND GINGER MOUSSE

For the meringue:
3 egg whites
6 oz (175g) raw cane sugar
good pinch of sea salt

2 bananas
2 oz (50g) stem ginger
6 egg yolks
7 egg whites
good pinch of sea salt
¾ pt (425 ml) whipping cream
4 oz (100g) raw cane sugar
¼ pt (140 ml) water

Make the meringues. First get any lumps out of the sugar with a pestle or a rolling pin; then sieve it. Whip the egg whites with salt until they stand up in peaks, then whisk in half of the sugar. Continue to whisk until shiny. Fold in the remaining sugar, and spoon onto a lightly oiled baking sheet. Place in a cool oven 250°F/130°C (Gas Mark ½) for two hours. When the meringues are ready, crumble them coarsely and set aside.

Slice the bananas very finely – big chunks of banana will end up like lumps of rubber in the ice cream. Slice the stem ginger into slivers.

Make the ice cream according to the basic recipe. Just before packing, fold in the banana and ginger, and lastly fold in the meringue, which should be in large enough chunks to be crunchy. If you crush it too finely the meringue will just vanish and all you will have is an added sweetness, rather than a crunchy contrast to the smooth ice cream.

ICED BLACKBERRY MOUSSE

For the purée:
2 lb (900g) blackberries
3 fl oz (80ml) water
¼ pt (140ml) heavy syrup (made with 1 lb (450g) sugar and ¼ pt (140ml) water)
2½ fl oz (70ml) lemon juice

6 egg yolks
7 egg whites
4 oz (100g) sugar
¼ pt (140ml) water
¾ pt (425ml) whipping cream

To make the blackberry *purée*, cook the blackberries over a low heat with 3 fl oz water to extract the juice. When soft, remove from the heat. Place in a liquidizer and *purée* with the heavy syrup. Add the lemon juice to taste. Sieve the *purée* if you don't like pips. You should end up with approximately 1-1¼ pints of *purée*. Set aside.

Make the ice cream according to the basic recipe for this section, and add the blackberry *purée* just before you add the whipped cream.

ICED BLACKCURRANT MOUSSE

For the purée:
2 lb (900g) blackcurrants
¼ pt (140ml) heavy syrup (made with 1 lb (450g) sugar and ¼ pt (140ml) water)

6 egg yolks
7 egg whites
4 oz (100g) sugar
¼ pt (140ml) water
¾ pt (425ml) whipping cream

This mousse is best made with raw blackcurrants. Top and tail them, then liquidize them with the heavy syrup, a little at a time. Sieve if you don't like pips.

Make up the ice cream according to the basic recipe and add the blackcurrant *purée* just before you add the whipped cream.

ICED BROWN BREAD MOUSSE

6 egg yolks
7 egg whites
4 oz (100g) light muscovado sugar
¼ pt (140ml) water
¾ pt (425ml) whipping cream
pinch of sea salt
2 oz (50g) brown breadcrumb mixture (see section on Stores)

Make up the ice cream according to the basic recipe and fold in the brown breadcrumb mixture just before packing; then freeze as quickly as possible to stop the crumbs becoming soggy.

ICED FUDGE MOUSSE

2 oz (50g) chopped fudge (see section on Stores)
6 egg yolks
7 egg whites
4 oz (100g) light muscovado sugar
¼ pt (140ml) water
¾ pt (425ml) whipping cream
pinch of sea salt

Make up the ice cream according to the basic recipe and fold in the chopped fudge just before packing; then freeze as quickly as possible.

ICED GOOSEBERRY MOUSSE

For the purée:
1½ lb (675g) gooseberries
4oz (100g) (4 tablespoonsful) honey
4 tablespoonsful water

6 egg yolks
7 egg whites
4oz (100g) light muscovado sugar
¼pt (140ml) water
¾pt (425ml) whipping cream

Cook the gooseberries over a low heat with the water until soft. Stir in the honey. Liquidize and set aside to cool.

Make up the ice cream according to the basic method for this section. Beat in the gooseberry *purée* just before you add the whipped cream. Chill and freeze.

Variations:
1. At the final beating, fold in three roughly crushed meringues. Pack and freeze.
2. Use ¼ pint elderflower syrup (see Stores section) in place of honey.

ICED HONEY MOUSSE

4 eggs
4oz (100g) mild honey (warmed)
1 grated lemon rind
1 grated orange rind
¼pt (140ml) cream
juice of 1 lemon

Separate the eggs. Beat the egg yolks and honey together until pale and creamy. Add the lemon and orange rind and the lemon juice. Whisk the cream until thick and fold this into the mixture. Fold in the whisked egg whites. Chill and freeze.

ICED ORANGE MOUSSE

½ 6 fl oz (165 ml) tin concentrated unsweetened orange juice
1 oz (25g) raisins, soaked overnight in 2 fl oz (55 ml) orange juice or
brandy
2 oz (50g) candied orange peel
6 egg yolks
7 egg whites
4 oz (100g) raw cane sugar
¼ pt (140 ml) water
¾ pt (425 ml) whipping cream

Make the ice cream according to the basic recipe. Just before adding
the whipped cream, beat in the concentrated orange juice. At the final
beating add the raisins and candied orange peel.

ICED PRALINE MOUSSE

6 egg yolks
7 egg whites
4 oz (100g) light muscovado sugar
¼ pt (140 ml) water
¾ pt (425 ml) whipping cream
pinch of sea salt
2 oz (50g) praline (see Stores section)

Make up the ice cream according to the basic recipe for this section
and fold in the praline just before packing; then freeze as quickly as
possible.

Variation: This recipe is for a crunchy praline mixture. If you prefer your
praline pounded to a paste, add it to the egg yolk and syrup mixture
before you add the cream and egg whites. If you use this method, you
will not need to beat the ice cream before the final packing.

ICED QUINCE MOUSSE

For the purée:
2 lb (900g) quinces
4 oz (100g) apples
4 oz (100g) honey
rind and juice of 1 lemon
½ pt (275ml) water

6 egg yolks
7 egg whites
4 oz (100g) light muscovado sugar
¼ pt (140ml) water
¾ pt (425ml) whipping cream

Make a *purée* from the quinces, apples, honey and lemon as for quince sherbet (see chapter 5). Make the ice cream according to the recipe. Just before adding the whipped cream add the *purée*.

Variation: Reserve two of the quinces. Poach these whole in a syrup of 4 oz raw cane sugar and ¼ pint water. When tender but still firm, remove from the syrup. Cool, core and slice thinly. Coat them with honey and add to the ice cream just before packing for the final freezing.

ICED RASPBERRY MOUSSE

For the purée:
1½ lb (675g) raspberries
2½ fl oz (70ml) water
4 oz (100g) mild honey
good squeeze of lemon juice

6 egg yolks
7 egg whites
4 oz (100g) raw cane sugar
¼ pt (140ml) water
¾ pt (425ml) cream

Reserve 2 oz of raspberries whole, sprinkle them with 1 dessertspoonful of honey and set aside. Dissolve the rest of the honey in the water. Allow to cool. *Purée* the rest of the raspberries in a liquidizer or sieve with the honey, water and the lemon juice.

Make the ice cream according to the recipe, adding the raspberry *purée* just before the whipped cream. Just before packing, add the whole raspberries, being careful not to break them up.

ICED RUM AND RAISIN MOUSSE

This is good made with a blend of dark and light muscovado sugars.

3 oz (75g) large raisins
3 tablespoonsful dark rum
3 egg yolks
4 egg whites
2 oz (50g) dark muscovado sugar
2 oz (50g) light muscovado sugar
¼ pt (140ml) water
¾ pt (425ml) cream

Cut the raisins in half and pour the rum over them. Leave them to soak for one to two hours or overnight. Beat the yolks until light and foamy.

Boil the sugars and water together to the thread stage or until your sugar thermometer registers 220°F, then pour the syrup in a steady stream over the egg yolks, beating all the time. Continue beating until the mixture is thick and creamy. Cool, then add the whipped cream. Whip the egg whites and fold in. Chill and freeze. Before packing, fold in the rum and raisins, then freeze again.

ICED MOUSSES WITH WINE – 'Semi-freddi'

Alcohol, like sugar, makes ice creams freeze less hard. This means that you will be able to eat them straight from the freezer without leaving them half an hour in the refrigerator to soften. If you happen to be a maker of country wines you have a whole range of exotic ices within your power. Here are one classic Italian and two English country variations.

ZABAGLIONE (Serves 4)

3 egg yolks
½ tablespoonful water
2 oz (50g) sugar
4 fl oz (110ml) Marsala
6 fl oz (165ml) cream

Combine egg yolks, water, sugar and Marsala in the top of a double boiler and beat over boiling water until thick and foamy. Remove from the heat and continue beating until cool. Chill. Whip the cream and fold in. Pack and freeze.

Ices incorporating wine or spirits are known in Italy as 'semi-freddi' because they never freeze really hard.

Variations:
1. Instead of Marsala, try ¼ pint elderflower wine.
2. Replace the Marsala with ¼ pint ginger wine and serve sprinkled with chopped stem ginger.

Note: Allow a little extra time for ices with alcohol, as they take longer to freeze, and do not add more than the recommended quantity or they may separate.

3. An increasing number of country wines are available in wholefood shops, and these lend themselves very well to this kind of ice. Try apple, elderflower, gooseberry or elderberry.

SEMI-FREDDO WITH MEAD (Serves 4)

3 egg yolks
½ tablespoonful water
2 oz (50g) honey
4 fl oz (110ml) mead
6 fl oz (165ml) cream

Put egg yolks, water, honey and mead in the top of a double boiler and whisk over boiling water until thick and foamy. Remove from the heat and continue beating until cool. Whip the cream until firm and fold into the egg mixture. Chill, pack and freeze.

PARFAITS

The same mixture and method which is used to make an iced mousse is also used for parfaits. The difference is in the presentation and the mouthwatering combinations you can create. Approximate amounts which the recipes for iced mousses will produce are given at the beginning of the section. These will almost certainly be more than you need for a parfait, so first decide on the flavour you want, then decide how many people you wish to feed, and lastly pick your mould and make sure it will hold the right quantity. As a rough guide, 1 pint will feed four people, 2 pints will feed seven to eight.

Any ice cream left over from your batch can be packed and stored for everyday eating. Recipes for the sauces mentioned will be found in the section on sauces and toppings.

1. *Apple and Honey Parfait* Freeze in a mould. Turn out and decorate with whipped cream and toasted hazelnuts. Serve with fudge sauce.

2. *Apricot and Almond Parfait* Freeze in a ring mould. Turn out and fill the centre with stewed apricots and sprinkle with flaked toasted almonds. Alternatively, pour over apricot and orange sauce and sprinkle grated carob bar over the top.

3. *Banana Parfait* Freeze in a mould. Turn out and decorate with chopped stem ginger and whipped cream. Serve with maple syrup.

4. *Blackcurrant Parfait* Freeze in a mould. Turn out and decorate with whipped cream. Pour over blackcurrant sauce and sprinkle with toasted sunflower seeds.

5. *Brown Bread Parfait* Freeze in a mould or *soufflé* dish. Turn out and decorate with whipped cream, and pour over raspberry sauce or spiced plum sauce.

6. *Chestnut Parfait* Freeze in a *soufflé* dish or mould. Turn out and decorate with whipped cream and grated carob. Serve with chestnut or carob sauce.

7. *Gooseberry Parfait* Freeze in a mould. Unmould and decorate with grapes, halved and pipped, and whipped cream. Serve with elderflower syrup.

8. *Hazelnut Parfait* Freeze in a ring mould. Turn out and fill the centre

with fresh loganberries and decorate with tiny hazelnut meringues. Alternatively, pour over a raspberry sauce and decorate with whipped cream and whole toasted hazelnuts.

9. *Orange Parfait* Freeze in a mould. Turn out and serve decorated with orange segments, sprinkled with praline and accompanied by Burnt Orange Sauce.

10. *Praline Parfait* Freeze in a mould. Turn out, decorate with whipped cream and flaked toasted almonds and serve with spiced plum or loganberry sauce.

11. *Prune Parfait* Freeze in a mould. Turn out and decorate with whipped cream flavoured with rum and cashew nuts. Serve with a hot orange sauce.

12. *Raspberry Parfait* Freeze in a mould. Turn out, decorate with fresh raspberries and whipped cream and serve with a redcurrant sauce.

13. *Rum and Raisin Parfait* Freeze in a mould. Turn out and decorate with whipped cream and chopped nuts. Serve with rich raisin sauce.

14. *Strawberry Parfait* Freeze in a ring mould. Turn out, fill the centre with fresh strawberries in redcurrant sauce. Decorate with whipped cream.

4. Iced Creams and Soufflés

The earliest ice creams in England in the seventeenth century were precisely this – cream frozen with a *purée* of fruit; in other words, a sort of frozen fruit fool. This is a very quick, easy and extravagant way of making ice cream. Made with a fruit as rich and rare as the mulberry, it offers a high spot in summer eating.

1 lb (450g) mulberries
6 oz (175g) light muscovado sugar
1 pt (550ml) whipping cream
juice of half a lemon

Liquidize the mulberries, reserving a few for garnish. Sieve them to remove the seeds. Add the sugar and lemon juice. Whip the cream until firm and fold in the mulberry *purée*. Chill and freeze.

Variations: This is good with all soft fruits. Try it with fresh raw blackcurrants, *puréed* and sieved, strawberries, raspberries or loganberries.

Note: Remember that this type of ice cream will freeze fairly hard, and will need at least thirty minutes in the refrigerator to soften before you serve it. The addition of beaten egg white will make it lighter and easier to soften.

APRICOT ICED CREAM (Serves 4-6)

4 oz (100g) dried apricots
½ pt (275ml) water
4 oz (100g) honey
2 egg whites
1 tablespoonful marmalade
½ pt (275ml) whipping cream

Soak the apricots in the water overnight, then simmer them with the water, honey and marmalade. Cool and liquidize. You should have approximately ½ pint of *purée*. Fold in the stiffly whipped cream, and lastly the stiffly beaten egg whites. Chill and freeze.

Note: The basic recipe has been altered by the addition of two egg whites to lighten this ice cream.

ELDERBERRY ICED CREAM (Serves 6-8)

1 pt (550ml) elderberries
¼ pt (140ml) red grape juice
4 oz (100g) honey
squeeze of lemon juice
¾ pt (425ml) cream
2½ fl oz (70ml) port or elderberry wine – optional

Simmer the elderberries with honey, grape juice, and lemon juice. Make a *purée*, and add the port if liked. Check for taste. Whip the cream until firm and fold in the elderberry *purée*. Chill and freeze.

MAPLE SYRUP BOMBE (Serves 6)

This is not really a bombe, but sweetened cream with meringue, lightly frozen in a mould.

½ pt (275ml) whipping cream
maple syrup to taste
8 meringues, halved (see Stores section)
stem ginger or raspberries to garnish

Oil a 1½ pint mould. Break the meringues into three or four pieces. Whip the crem lightly and sweeten to taste with maple syrup. Add the cream to the meringues and mix gently. Fill the mould and freeze. To serve, put the mould into a bowl of warm water for a few seconds, slip a knife round the rim to loosen it and turn out onto a chilled plate. Soften for about 40 minutes in the refrigerator. Serve topped with chopped stem ginger or surrounded with raspberries.

ICED SOUFFLÉS

An iced *soufflé* is made with syrup, flavouring, whipped cream and egg whites. If you have been making ice cream following the mousse method, it is a good way of using the egg whites you may have over. Fruit ice creams made this way are delicious.

Basic recipe:
4oz (100g) raw cane sugar
¼ pt (140ml) water
2 egg whites
pinch of sea salt
½ pt (275ml) fruit purée
¼·½ pt (140·275ml) whipped cream

Heat the sugar and water in a pan until the sugar dissolves, then boil fast for five minutes, watching so that it does not boil over. Whisk the egg whites stiffly with the salt then pour the hot syrup over them in a steady stream, whisking all the time until the mixture is thick. Cool this meringue mixture by standing the bowl in cold water or in a bowl of ice cubes. Whisk from time to time.

Whip the cream, but not too stiffly. Fold the fruit into the whipped cream and add the meringue mixture. Chill and freeze.

This does not need to be beaten half way like a custard-based ice cream.

Note: It is useful to have a metal bowl for this type of ice cream. The egg whites will whisk more easily and the meringue mixture will cool more quickly than in a china or plastic bowl.

ICED LEMON SOUFFLÉ (Serves 4)

3 oz (75g) light muscovado sugar
3 egg whites
¼ pt (140ml) water
juice of 2 lemons
pared rind of 1 lemon
¼ pt (140ml) whipping cream

Heat the sugar and water with the lemon rind until the sugar dissolves, then boil fast for five minutes. Whisk the egg whites until firm. Strain the syrup over the egg whites as for basic method. Allow to cool. Whip the cream and add the lemon juice to it. Fold the cream into the meringue mixture and freeze.

Variations:
1. Instead of lemons, use limes for a beautifully sharp and refreshing ice.
2. Instead of the juice of two lemons, add ¼ pint dry white wine.

ICED LOGANBERRY SOUFFLÉ (Serves 6-8)

4 oz (100g) light muscovado sugar
¼ pt (140ml) water
2 egg whites
¾ lb (425ml) fresh loganberries
¼ pt (140ml) whipping cream

Purée the loganberries, sieve them if you prefer. You should end up with ½ pint *purée.*

Follow the basic recipe for an iced *soufflé.* Add the *purée* to the meringue mixture before you add the whipped cream.

ICED ORANGE SOUFFLÉ (Serves 4-6)

3 oz (75g) light muscovado sugar
¼ pt (140ml) water
3 egg whites
juice and rind of 1 lemon
juice of 2 oranges
¼ pt (140ml) whipping cream

Follow basic method as for iced lemon *soufflé*.

Note: For a really strong tasting orange *soufflé*, use one third of a 6 fl oz (165ml) tin of frozen concentrated orange juice instead of the fresh orange juice.

5. Water Ices, Granitas, Sorbets and Sherbets

Many people are confused by the different names given to water ices. Basically, they are all syrups flavoured in a number of ways, but principally with fruit juices or *purées*, and treated in slightly different ways during freezing.

Water Ices are just syrup with sweetened fruit juice, sometimes with wine or liqueur added. The mixture is stirred or beaten several times during freezing. The mixture will freeze from the outside inwards so it is important to fork the frozen edges to the middle every half hour or so to ensure even freezing.

Granitas are basically the same mixture, but they are frozen without beating. They are stirred lightly and served in a mushy slightly grainy state. Commercial manufacturers of ices in Great Britain can now buy something called a slush machine which produces aptly translated granitas. If you are making granitas to store and serve later, freeze without stirring. The stirring can all be done during the thawing process before you serve it.

Sorbets are water ices to which is added a little egg white. These are well beaten half-way through the freezing stage, and at this point you add the egg white, which will lighten the texture of the finished ice and prevent it from freezing too hard. The finished sorbet should be smooth and fairly firm — about the consistency of firm snow.

The term *Sherbet* is one over which there is a certain amount of confusion. In the East it has always meant an iced drink based on sweetened fruit juice. In this country the term is used to describe a sweet much beloved of small children, which comes in powder form

and is sucked through a straw, to fizz on the tongue. In the United
States it seems to have two further meanings. It is sometimes used as
another name for a water ice, and sometimes for a water ice to which
milk or cream has been added. For the purposes of this book, a sherbet
is a water ice to which a little whipped cream has been added.

WATER ICES AND GRANITAS

Basic recipe:
1 pt (550ml) water
10 oz (275g) mild honey or raw cane sugar
flavouring

Bring the honey and water to the boil and boil for five minutes to make the syrup. It will boil up and over unless you are around to keep an eye on it, so choose a large saucepan, and stir it or blow on it to stop it boiling over. Cool the syrup and add the flavouring. Chill and freeze. Remember that an ice containing too little sugar will freeze rock hard and be difficult to serve, too much and it will be difficult to freeze.

Freezing directions for water ices: Freeze to a mush, stirring the outsides to the middle with a fork from time to time. When the mush is becoming firm beat thoroughly until the texture is quite smooth. Pack and freeze.

Freezing directions for granitas: If you are making it to eat at once, stir lightly with a fork every half hour or so, bringing the frozen edges into the middle. When it is mushy, serve, preferably in long glasses. The freezing process will take two or three hours. If you are making it to store and eat later, freeze without touching it. When you want to serve it, thaw for about two hours, forking lightly from time to time.

Most fruits can be turned into a delicious water ice or granita. Either extract the juice by gentle simmering, or liquidize raw fruit. Either way, you will need 3/4 pint of pulp or juice to 1/4 pint of syrup to make enough for four people.

Most of the recipes for water ices and granitas are for fruit-flavoured syrups, but delectable ices can be made with syrup flavoured with coffee, tea or wine.

In some of the following recipes I have suggested the addition of agar agar if you wish to turn the syrup into a water ice. This will help to produce a smoother, firmer ice, but the flavoured syrup must be brought to the boil to dissolve the agar agar, so if you want to make your ice with raw fruit, omit it.

Quantities are for four to six people unless otherwise stated.

BLACKCURRANT WINE GRANITA

½pt (275ml) blackcurrant wine
4oz (100g) honey
½pt (275ml) water
juice and peel of 1 lemon

Boil the honey, lemon peel and water together for five minutes to make the syrup. Cool, strain and add the lemon juice and blackcurrant wine. Chill, and freeze to a granita.

Variation: Use dandelion wine instead of blackcurrant for a delicious gold sparkling dessert.

COFFEE GRANITA

1pt (550ml) strong fresh coffee
5oz (150g) light muscovado sugar
½ teaspoonful agar agar – optional for water ices

This is best made with fresh coffee, using 4 tablespoonsful of freshly ground coffee to a pint of water. If you are making a water ice and like to add agar agar, bring the coffee to the boil and sprinkle on the agar agar, then stir to dissolve. Add the sugar to the hot coffee and stir until it is dissolved. Cool, chill and freeze.

Variation: Instead of light muscovado sugar, use 5oz of maple syrup – delicious. Serve with whipped cream.

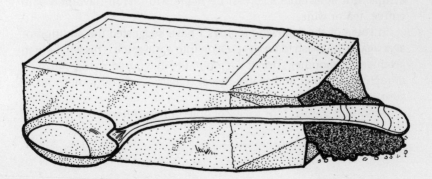

GRAPE GRANITA

From time to time, you will find cheap grapes in the shops – September is the month to look out for these. We have a vine growing on the side of the house which produces sour little green grapes, perfect for this recipe but not for anything else. Failing all else, use bottled grape juice. The method will vary accordingly.

If you use the muscatel grapes which are often available in September, the best way to treat them is to liquidize them raw, then strain.

If your grapes are like ours, home-grown with tough skins, you will have to stew them very gently with $2\frac{1}{2}$ fl oz water to extract the juice.

½ pt (275ml) water
4 oz (100g) mild honey
¼ pt (140ml) bottled grape juice or 1 lb (450g) grapes
juice of ½ lemon
juice of ½ orange

Make a syrup by boiling the honey and water together for five minutes. Allow to cool then add this to the grape juice with the orange and lemon juice. Cool, chill and freeze according to the basic method.

Variation: Add 3 tablespoonsful elderflower wine instead of orange juice.

STRAWBERRY GRANITA

1 ¼ lb (550g) strawberries to make 1 pt (550ml) juice
¼ pt (140ml) red grape juice
4 oz (100g) honey
¼ pt (140ml) water
juice of 1 lemon

Liquidize the strawberries with the red grape juice or push them through a sieve. Make a syrup by boiling the honey and water together for five minutes. Allow to cool. Mix the syrup with the strawberry juice and the lemon juice and freeze without stirring.

To serve, thaw to a mush, breaking up with a fork from time to time. Serve in glasses.

Variation: Use redcurrant juice instead of red grape juice, to give this granita extra bite and a lovely colour.

ICED TEA GRANITA

3 level teaspoonsful Earl Grey tea
1pt (550ml) water
6oz (175g) honey
rind of 2 lemons
juice of 3 lemons

Put the water, honey and lemon rind in a saucepan. Dissolve the honey completely, then boil fast for five to six minutes. Take off the heat and add the tea-leaves. Cover and infuse for half an hour. Add the lemon juice. Strain, chill and freeze without stirring.

    To serve, thaw to a mush, and serve in glasses.

Note: This quantity of tea-leaves produces a refreshing, slightly bitter ice that is not to everyone's taste. Use less if you prefer it milder.

Variations: Experiment with other scented teas such as gunpowder green tea, Keemun, Lapsang Suchong or Jasmine.

WATERMELON GRANITA

½ a ripe 3lb (1k 350g) watermelon
4oz (100g) honey
squeeze of lemon juice

The stripey watermelons always seem to have the best flavour. A 3lb watermelon ought to give you about 1½ pints of pulp.

    Remove the skin and pips and cut up the pulp. Liquidize it with the honey and measure ¾ pint of pulp. Add the lemon juice and check for taste. Chill and freeze according to the basic method. This makes a lovely crisp pink ice.

DAMSON WATER ICE WITH SLOE GIN

1 lb (450g) damsons
¾ pt (425ml) water
6 oz (175g) light muscovado sugar
2 tablespoonsful sloe gin
½ teaspoonful agar agar

Stew the damsons in ½ pint water in a covered pan over a low heat to extract the juice for fifteen minutes. Mash roughly with a wooden spoon and then strain the mixture. Measure the juice. Top up to ¾ pint with water if necessary.

Make a syrup by boiling together the sugar and ¼ pint water for five minutes. Add the damson juice and the sloe gin to the syrup. Bring back to the boil and sprinkle on the agar agar. Stir briskly to dissolve. Cool, taste for sweetness and freeze according to basic method for water ice.

Note: If you wish to make a granita, omit the agar agar.

ELDERBERRY WATER ICE WITH PORT

¾ pt (425ml) elderberry juice
juice and rind of 1 lemon
4 oz (100g) light muscovado sugar
¼ pt (140ml) water
¼ pt (140ml) port or elderberry wine
½ teaspoonful agar agar

You will need a good bag of elderberries to get ¾ pint of juice. Strip the berries from the stalk with a fork, and stew them with just enough water to cover the bottom of the pan, mashing them from time to time to extract the juice. Strain and measure.

Place the lemon rind with the sugar and water in a saucepan. Dissolve completely then boil fast for five or six minutes. Add to the elderberry juice with the wine and the lemon juice. Bring to the boil, sprinkle on the agar agar and stir to dissolve. Cool, chill, then taste for sweetness and add more lemon juice if necessary.

Freeze, forking the ice from the sides of the bowl to the middle from time to time. When it has frozen to a firm mush, remove from the freezer, beat thoroughly until smooth, pack and freeze.

SORBETS

Basic recipe:

1 pt (550 ml) fruit juice
½ pt (275 ml) water
6 oz (175 g) honey
1 egg white
lemon juice – optional

Dissolve the honey in the water in a large saucepan (be careful as the honey will boil up) then boil for five minutes. Cool the syrup and add to the fruit juice or *purée*. Set aside to cool. Taste, and add lemon juice if you like. Sorbets must at this stage be sweeter than you might like. Always remember to allow for the fact that freezing will diminish the flavour, so make it strong. Chill, and freeze to a mush, forking the sides to the middle from time to time. This will take three or four hours.

Now whisk the egg whites in a big bowl until stiff. Add the ice to it a little at a time, whisking with a hand whisk until pale and foamy. There are different schools of thought as to how the egg white should be added. Some people add the egg white, lightly broken up, to the chilled syrup before adding it to the fruit juice. You must see which method you prefer.

Pack and freeze until firm, but not rock hard. It will take three to four hours in the freezer before a water ice is firm enough to be beaten with the egg white and turned into a sorbet, and another one to two hours until it is the consistency of firm snow, and ready to serve.

BILBERRY SORBET

2 lb (900g) bilberries
1/4 pt (140ml) water
1/2 pt (275ml) red grape juice
4 oz (100g) honey
1/2 teaspoonful agar agar

Simmer the bilberries gently with the red grape juice and water to extract the juice for thirty minutes. Strain and measure – you should have approximately 1 1/4 pints. Put it back in the saucepan with the honey. Bring to the boil slowly, stirring to dissolve the honey. When boiling, sprinkle on the agar agar, stirring briskly to dissolve, then set aside to cool. Chill and freeze. Taste for sweetness. When frozen to a mush, add the stiffly whipped egg white, little by little. Pack and freeze.

Note: The agar agar in this recipe will prevent the syrup and the egg white from separating in the final freezing process.

BLACKBERRY SORBET

1 1/2 lb (675g) blackberries
1/2 pt (275ml) water
6 oz (175g) honey
juice of 1/2 lemon
1/2 teaspoonful agar agar
1 egg white

Simmer the blackberries with 1/4 pint water and the lemon to extract the juice. Strain and measure. You should have 1 pint of juice. Dissolve the honey in 1/4 pint water and boil for five minutes. Add the blackberry juice and the lemon juice. Bring to the boil and sprinkle on the agar agar. Whisk thoroughly to dissolve, then set aside to cool. Chill and freeze.

When mushy, stir ice into one stiffly beaten egg white in a large bowl. Whisk until smooth, pack and freeze.

BLACKCURRANT SORBET

1 ¼ lb (550g) blackcurrants
¼ pt (140ml) water
6 oz (175g) honey
juice of ½ lemon
½ egg white

Simmer the blackcurrants gently for five minutes with ¼ pint water. Dissolve the honey in the water and boil for five minutes. Cool, then liquidize the blackcurrant *purée* with the lemon juice and the honey syrup. Sieve, chill and freeze to a mushy state. Beat or liquidize, stir in the egg white, pack and return to the freezer.

Note: In this recipe I have suggested liquidizing the ice instead of whisking by hand at the final beating. If you do this you will have a very fine textured sorbet, but you must pack and freeze it very quickly.

CRAB APPLE SORBET

½ pt (275ml) apple juice
½ pt (275ml) water
1 ½ lb (675g) crab apples
3 tablespoonsful concentrated apple juice
3 tablespoonsful honey
½ teaspoonful agar agar – optional
1 egg white, stiffly whipped

Simmer the crab apples with the apple juice and water until soft and pulpy, to extract the juice. This will take approximately ten minutes. Strain, mashing the pulp with a wooden spoon to get as much of the juice as possible. You should have 1 pint of juice. If not, make up to 1 pint with water.

Return to the pan with the concentrated apple juice and honey. Stir to dissolve the honey. Bring to the boil, sprinkle on the agar agar and stir briskly to dissolve. Boil for a minute. Cool and freeze according to the directions for sorbets. When nearly firm, beat in the stiffly whipped white of egg. Pack and return to the freezer.

DAMSON SORBET

1½ lb (675g) damsons
½ pt (275ml) water
6 oz (175g) raw cane sugar
½ teaspoonful agar agar – optional
1 egg white

Stew the damsons with sugar and water until soft. Sprinkle on the agar agar and stir well to dissolve. Cool, remove the stones and liquidize the pulp.

Freeze to a mushy state, then remove from the freezer. Whip the egg white. Beat the sorbet, to break up the ice crystals, or liquidize. Add the beaten egg white. Pack and freeze.

ELDERBERRY AND PORT SORBET

2 lb (900g) elderberries
½ pt (275ml) red grape juice
4 oz (100g) honey
¼ pt (140ml) port or port-type wine
juice of ½ lemon
1 teaspoonful agar agar
1 egg white

Stew the elderberries gently with 2 tablespoonsful of water to extract the juice. Strain and measure – you should have ¾ pint. Dissolve the honey in the red grape juice and add to the elderberry juice, with the port and the lemon juice. Bring to the boil and sprinkle on the agar agar, stirring well to dissolve. Set aside to cool. Taste, and add more lemon if you like.

Freeze to a mush and then beat. Add the whipped egg white, pack and freeze. This sorbet will never freeze really hard, because of the alcohol, so you can serve it straight from the freezer.

ELDERFLOWER SORBET MADE WITH SYRUP

1 pt elderflower syrup (see Stores Section)
1 egg white

Freeze the elderflower syrup to a mush. Whisk the egg white until stiff and then add this to the syrup. Beat until smooth. Pack and freeze.

GRAPEFRUIT SORBET

½ pt (275 ml) water
6 oz (175g) honey
pared rind and juice of 1 large lemon
1½ tubs (9 fl oz) frozen concentrated grapefruit juice
1 egg white

Put pared lemon rind in a saucepan with the honey and water. Bring to the boil, stirring to dissolve the honey. Boil for five minutes and leave to cool.

Remove the lemon rind, and add the grapefruit and lemon juices. Chill and freeze to a mush. Remove from the freezer, beat until smooth, then quickly fold in the stiffly whisked egg white. Pack and freeze.

This looks pretty made with pink Texas grapefruit.

Variation: **GRAPEFRUIT WITH MINT**
Take a good handful of mint leaves stripped from the stalks. When you take the honey and water syrup off the heat, plunge in the mint leaves and leave covered to infuse for twenty minutes. Strain onto the grapefruit and lemon juice and proceed as for the previous recipe. A lemon mint is very good for this sorbet.

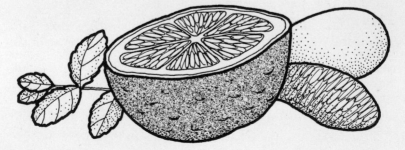

HONEY SORBET

½ lb (225g) honey
1 pt (550ml) water
juice of 1 lemon
½ teaspoonful agar agar
1 egg white

Dissolve the honey in the water with the lemon juice. Bring to the boil and sprinkle on the agar agar. Stir to dissolve. Set aside to cool. Freeze to a mush, then add the beaten egg white and finish freezing according to directions for sorbets.

Note: There is a wide choice of honeys on the market. Try experimenting with different flavours.

Variation 1: To give an unusual flavour try adding your favourite herb. After you have added the agar agar, plunge in a handful of fresh lemon balm or tansy which you have previously bruised with a pestle and mortar (a piece of 2in. x 2in. hardwood and a plastic bucket will do just as well for this operation). Leave to cool in the saucepan with the lid on for half an hour. Strain and freeze to a mush. Beat in the egg white, pack and return to freezer.

Variation 2: Add a good pinch of cinnamon and nutmeg to the honey and lemon mixture.

LEMON SORBET

1 pt (550ml) water
6 oz (175g) mild honey
pared rind and juice of 3 lemons – to make ¼ pt (140ml) juice
1 egg white

Put the lemon rind, honey and water in a saucepan. Bring to the boil, stirring to dissolve the honey. Boil for five minutes. Remove from the heat then stir in the lemon juice. Allow to cool and then strain. Chill and freeze to a mush.

Remove from the freezer and beat until smooth. Fold in the stiffly whisked egg white. Pack and freeze.

LIME SORBET

1 pt (550 ml) water
peel and juice of 6 fresh limes – to make ¼ pt (140 ml) juice
6 oz (175 g) honey
1 egg white

Put the lime peel, water and honey in a saucepan and bring to the boil. Boil briskly for five minutes. Cool, strain and add the lime juice. Chill and freeze to a mush.

Remove from the freezer, beat in the stiffly whisked egg white. Pack and freeze.

Variation: Replace ½ pint water with ½ pint white grape juice.

MANDARIN SORBET

8 oz (225 g) *puréed* mandarins, tinned in natural juices or fresh
6 oz (175 g) mild honey
¾ pt (425 ml) water
1 tablespoonful concentrated frozen orange juice
juice and rind of 1 lemon
1 egg white

Liquidize the mandarins. Dissolve the honey in the water over a low heat, with the lemon rind. Bring to the boil and boil briskly for five minutes. Cool, strain and add the mandarin *purée*, lemon juice and concentrated orange juice. Freeze to a mush. Whisk the egg white until stiff. Add the egg white to the sorbet, beat until smooth. Pack and freeze.

Variation: This can also be made with tangerines or satsumas.

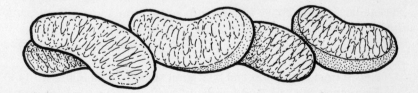

MELON SORBET

1½-2 lb (675-900g) melon
4 oz (100g) honey
¼ pt (140ml) water
3-4 tablespoonsful lemon juice
1 rounded teaspoonful ground ginger – optional
1 egg white

A 1½-2 lb melon should give you about 1 pint of pulp. Dissolve the honey in the water over a moderate heat. Remove the melon seeds, spoon out the pulp and liquidize with the ginger and the honey syrup. Add the lemon juice to taste, chill and freeze. Add the egg white according to directions and finish freezing.

To serve, top with chopped stem ginger.

Note: The ginger in this recipe is optional. If you prefer to leave it out, you might try adding a small pinch of white pepper, which will bring out the flavour of the melon.

NECTARINE SORBET (Serves 8-10)

6 nectarines
1 lb (450g) mild honey
1 pt (550ml) water
1 egg white

This is simple to make and quite delicious. Pick good sized nectarines with dark red skins.

Dissolve the honey in the water and boil for five minutes. Remove from the heat. Stone the nectarines, quarter them and drop the quarters immediately into the hot syrup. Allow to cool, then liquidize, chill and freeze. When nearly firm, beat into the stiffly whisked egg white, pack and finish freezing.

ORANGE SORBET

6 oz (175g) honey
¾ pt (425 ml) water
rind of 1 lemon and 1 orange, in strips
1½ cans (9 fl oz) frozen concentrated orange juice
1 egg white

Dissolve the honey in the water. Add the lemon and orange rinds and boil for five minutes. Allow to cool, then strain onto the concentrated orange juice, mix well and chill. Check the taste.

Freeze to a mush, then add the stiffly beaten egg white. Whisk until it is thick, pack and freeze.

Note: This can also be made with fresh oranges, in which case, use only ½ pint water, and instead of the concentrated orange juice, use the juice of six oranges and one lemon, to make up ¾ pint juice.

ORANGE AND PASSION FRUIT SORBET

6 oz (175g) honey
½ pt (275 ml) water
6 fl oz (165 ml) orange juice
6 fl oz (165 ml) passion fruit juice
juice and rind of 1 large lemon
1 egg white

Put the lemon rind, honey and water into a pan over a low heat and bring to the boil, stirring to dissolve the honey. Boil for five minutes. Allow to cool, then strain the syrup into the juice of the oranges, passion fruit and lemon. Chill, then freeze to a mush. Remove from the freezer, beat until thick and smooth. Add the stiffly beaten egg white and return to the freezer.

PEACH SORBET (Serves 8-10)

This is best made with fresh peaches. The second best is canned white peaches in natural juices.

1½ lb (625g) peaches
¼ pt (140ml) white grape juice
12 oz (350g) honey
¾ pt (425ml) water
juice of 1 lemon
1 egg white

Boil the honey with the grape juice and the water for five minutes, then remove from the heat. Peel and stone the peaches and combine them with the syrup and lemon juice in the liquidizer. Chill, taste and freeze to a mush. Add the stiffly whisked egg white, pack and finish freezing.

Note: If you are using tinned peaches, replace some of the water with the juice from the tin.

PEAR SORBET

2 lb (900g) pears — preferably 1 lb (450g) cooking pears, 1 lb (450g) dessert pears, peeled and cored
½ pt apple juice
juice of 2 lemons
6 oz (175g) honey
½ teaspoonful agar agar
1 egg white

Pear sorbet can be insipid if made only with dessert pears, which is why I recommend using half cooking pears and half dessert.

Peel and core the pears and drop quickly into the apple juice to stop them discolouring. Add the honey and lemon juice and bring to the boil. Simmer gently for seven minutes, or until tender. Add the agar agar, stirring to dissolve, then liquidize. Allow to cool, taste, and add more lemon juice if liked, then freeze.

When mushy, remove from the freezer and liquidize or beat up with a whisk. Add the stiffly whipped egg white, pack and finish freezing.

RASPBERRY AND REDCURRANT SORBET (Serves 8-10)

1 1/4 lb (550g) raspberries
3/4 lb (350g) redcurrants
6 oz (175g) honey
1/2 pt (275ml) water
1 egg white

Boil the honey and water together for five minutes, then allow to cool. Meanwhile, simmer the redcurrants gently with 2 tablespoonsful of water to extract the juice. You should have about 6 fl oz juice. *Purée* the fresh raspberries, the redcurrant juice and the syrup in the liquidizer. Chill and freeze to a mush. Add the stiffly whisked egg white, beat until smooth and finish freezing.

Note: It is well worth storing redcurrant juice in 1/2 pint blocks in your freezer for use in the winter.

RASPBERRY SORBET (Serves 8-10)

1 1/4 lb (550g) raspberries
1/2 pt (275ml) red grape juice
1 tablespoonful honey
juice of 1/2 lemon
1 egg white

Melt the honey in the grape juice. Liquidize the fresh raspberries. Add the grape juice, honey and lemon juice. Freeze to a mush, then beat. Add the whipped egg white, pack and freeze.

LOGANBERRY SORBET

Follow the recipe for raspberry sorbet, but increase the honey to 1 1/2 tablespoonsful, as loganberries have a sharper taste than raspberries.

Variation: Mulberry Sorbet
Use this recipe for a mulberry sorbet if you are lucky enough to have mulberries.

REDCURRANT SORBET

1½ lb (675g) redcurrants
½ pt (275ml) apple juice
1½ oz (40g) raw cane sugar
½ teaspoonful agar agar
1 egg white, whipped

Simmer the redcurrants over a very low heat in a covered pan, with 3 tablespoonsful of water, to extract the juice. Strain and set aside.

Dissolve the sugar in the apple juice. Add the redcurrant juice, bring to the boil, sprinkle on the agar agar and whisk to dissolve. Set aside to cool then chill and freeze to a mush. Liquidize, adding the stiffly whisked egg white at the same time. Pack and freeze.

STRAWBERRY SORBET (Serves 8)

1 lb (450g) strawberries
½ pt (275ml) red grape juice
2 tablespoonsful honey
juice of 1 orange
juice of 1 lemon
1 egg white

Melt the honey with the red grape juice, the orange juice and the lemon juice. Pulp the fresh strawberries either with a sieve or in a liquidizer and add to the honey and juices.

Freeze to a mush, then beat and add the whipped egg white. Pack and freeze.

Variation: Replace the orange juice with 2½ fl oz of redcurrant juice for a delicious clean crisp flavour.

SORBETS WITH INFUSIONS

The basis for many of these delicious sorbets is a lemon water ice.

1 pt (550ml) water

6 oz (175g) mild honey
rind and juice of 3 lemons

Put the thinly peeled lemon rind with the honey and water in a clean saucepan. Stir to dissolve the honey, then boil fast for five to six minutes. Set aside to cool. Add the lemon juice and strain, then chill and freeze.

To make a sorbet with an infusion, prepare the honey and water syrup as for the above recipe. Have ready two or three handfuls of your chosen herb leaves stripped from the stalks.

When you take the syrup from the heat, plunge in the leaves. Put the lid on the saucepan and leave to infuse off the heat till the syrup is well flavoured. This will take up to half an hour. To vary the strength of the infusion, add more or less of the herb, leaves, or flower petals, rather than leaving it infusing for too long. (I have left elderflowers infusing overnight and ended up with a black and bitter liquid which I had to throw away.)

When the infusion is ready, strain it, pressing the leaves with a wooden spoon to extract all the juice. Add the lemon juice, chill and freeze.

BLACKCURRANT LEAF SORBET

1 pt (550ml) water
6 oz (175g) honey
pared rind of 2 lemons
juice of 3 lemons
3-4 handfuls blackcurrant leaves
1 egg white

This is best made in May or June when the blackcurrant leaves are young and tender. To be safe, pick only garden blackcurrant leaves as commercially grown ones are subjected to all sorts of insecticidal sprays.

Prepare the syrup as for the lemon water ice. Boil fast for five minutes. Plunge in the blackcurrant leaves. Remove from the heat, cover the pan and leave to infuse until well flavoured – not less than half an hour. Strain off the syrup, squeezing the leaves well to extract all the juice. Add the lemon juice, chill and freeze.

EARL GREY SORBET

3 tablespoonsful Earl Grey tea, or Lapsang Suchong
1 pt (550ml) water
6 oz (175g) honey
rind of 2 lemons
juice of 3 lemons
1 egg white

Make up the lemon syrup, boil for five minutes then add 3 tablespoons-ful of Earl Grey or any strong and scented tea. Cover and infuse for half an hour. (Do not leave it too long or it will become bitter.)

    Strain, add the lemon juice, chill and freeze to a mush. Beat into the egg white and finish freezing.

ELDERFLOWER SORBET

5-6 heads of elderflowers
1 pt (550ml) water
6 oz (175g) honey
rind and juice of 3 lemons
1 egg white

Make a syrup as for lemon water ice. After boiling for five minutes, remove from the heat. Drop in the elderflowers, cover and leave to infuse until strongly flavoured (about half an hour). Strain the syrup, add the lemon juice and freeze. When nearly firm, beat in the stiffly whisked egg white. Return to the freezer.

    This has a delicious taste of muscatel grapes. Pick the elderflowers in the middle of the day, preferably in sunshine when they are fully opened. They flower in June and July and it is well worth picking plenty and drying them for use in the winter.

Note: You can also make this sorbet with dried elderflowers or with an elderflower syrup, for which you will find a recipe in the section on Stores.

GERANIUM LEAF SORBET

1pt (550ml) apple juice
3oz (75g) mild honey
12-15 scented geranium leaves
lemon juice to taste
1 egg white

Boil the apple juice with the geranium leaves in a covered pan for twenty minutes. Remove the leaves and discard. Add the honey and stir to dissolve. Add a little lemon juice to taste, being careful not to swamp the flavour of the geranium leaves. Chill and freeze. When nearly firm, add the egg white according to the directions for sorbets.

PEPPERMINT SORBET

Peppermint ice cream can easily be a little reminiscent of tooth paste or chewing gum, which is why we prefer peppermint sorbet, made with an infusion of peppermint leaves.

3-4 handfuls of peppermint leaves stripped from the stems
1pt (550ml) water
6oz (175g) mild honey
rind and juice of 3 lemons
oil of peppermint
1 egg white

Make up the lemon syrup. Boil for five minutes then remove from the heat. Plunge in the peppermint leaves, cover the pan, and leave to infuse for half an hour.

Strain the liquid, squeezing the leaves to extract all the flavour. Add the lemon juice and two drops of oil of peppermint. Chill and freeze.

Variation: **MINT**
Substitute garden mint for the peppermint.

ROSE PETAL SORBET

1 pt (550ml) white grape juice
6 oz (175g) mild honey
3-4 handfuls of old rose petals, preferably dark red
1 teaspoonful agar agar
4 tablespoonsful concentrated white grape juice
1 egg white

In a mortar or a strong bowl pound the rose petals with the concentrated grape juice to a pulp. Put the pulp in a muslin bag.

Dissolve the honey in the grape juice over a low heat and then boil fast for five minutes. Sprinkle on the agar agar, stirring briskly to dissolve, then boil for a further five minutes. Remove from the heat and plunge the muslin bag containing the rose petal pulp into the hot syrup. Cover the pan and leave for half an hour. Remove the bag, squeezing to extract all the flavour. Chill and freeze.

You can also make this with dried rose petals, available from shops supplying ingredients for home-made wines. Use approximately 1 ½ oz rose petals. The taste and scent will still be rare and exotic, but the sorbet will be a murky brown colour (unless you add a few drops of colouring) — not the lovely pink you get from fresh rose petals.

Place the dried rose petals in a muslin bag and proceed as for fresh rose petals.

SHERBETS

The basic method and recipe for a sherbet is the same as for a sorbet. The only difference is that you add whipped cream when you beat it up, instead of egg white.

1 pt (550ml) water
6 oz (175g) honey
flavouring — generally fruit juice or *purée*
3-5 fl oz (80-140ml) cream, stiffly whipped

Some people put the ice in a blender instead of giving it a final beating with a hand whisk. This saves trouble, but watch it carefully and pack it very quickly afterwards as it will soon turn sloppy.

GUAVA SHERBET

This is a delicious pale pink, delicately flavoured sherbet.

¾ pt (425 ml) guava pulp, fresh or canned
6 oz (175g) honey
½ pt (275 ml) water
juice of ½ a lemon
3 fl oz (80 ml) whipping cream

Boil the honey and water for five minutes. Remove from the heat.
    Add the guava pulp and lemon juice to taste. Chill, check the taste and freeze to a mush. Remove from the freezer, beat until smooth and fold in the stiffly whipped cream. Pack and freeze.

LIME SHERBET

rind and juice of 6 fresh limes – to make ¼ pt juice
1 pt (550 ml) water
6 oz (175g) honey
¼ pt (140 ml) cream

Put the lime peel, water and honey in a saucepan and bring to the boil. Boil for five minutes. Add the lime juice, then strain. Chill and freeze to a mush.
    Whip the cream stiffly. Remove the lime ice from the freezer and beat until smooth. Fold in the whipped cream, pack and freeze.

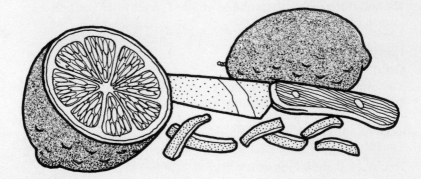

MANGO SHERBET

¾ pt (425ml) mango *purée*
½ pt (275ml) water
6 oz (175g) honey
¼ pt (140ml) cream
juice of ½-1 lemon

Either use fresh mangoes or mango cocktail. Dissolve the honey in the water and boil for five minutes. Allow to cool, then add the mango *purée* and the lemon juice to taste. Freeze to a mush, then beat and add the stiffly whipped cream. Pack and return to the freezer.

PASSION FRUIT SHERBET

¾ pt (425ml) passion fruit pulp or nectar
6 oz (175g) honey
½ pt (275ml) water
2½ fl oz (70 ml) whipped cream

Dissolve the honey in the water and boil for five minutes. Allow to cool then mix this with the passion fruit pulp. Chill and freeze to a mush. Beat in the stiffly whipped cream. Pack and freeze.

Variation: Passion Fruit and Orange Juice Sherbet
In place of water use orange juice.

PINEAPPLE SHERBET

1 pineapple – approx. 2 lb (900g) to yield ¾ pt (425ml) pulp
4 oz (100g) honey
½ pt (275g) water or white grape juice
2 tablespoonsful lemon juice
¼ pt (140ml) whipped cream

Cut the pineapple in half lengthwise, scoop out the flesh and cut away the core. Chop the flesh and liquidize roughly. Boil together the water or white grape juice and honey for five minutes. Mix with the pineapple pulp. Add lemon juice to taste, chill and freeze to a mush. Add the stiffly beaten egg white, then return to the freezer.

Note: To store for future special occasions, pile the sherbet into the half pineapple shell and wrap in clingfilm. Put in a polythene bag and freeze.

QUINCE SHERBET

This is a fruit which is hard to come by, but if you are lucky enough to have a quince tree or a friend with one, don't miss the chance to make this delicious and unusual sherbet in September.

2 lb (900g) quinces
4 oz (100g) apples
½ pt (275ml) water
4 oz (100g) honey
¼ pt (140ml) cream
zest and juice of one lemon
½ teaspoonful agar agar

Peel, core, and cut up the quinces and apples and simmer with the water, honey and lemon juice until pulpy. This may take some time as quinces are often slow to cook. Discard the lemon peel. Sprinkle on the agar agar and stir briskly to dissolve. Set aside to cool. Liquidize the pulp or put it through a sieve, adding more lemon if liked. Chill and freeze. When mushy, add the whipped cream. Pack and freeze.

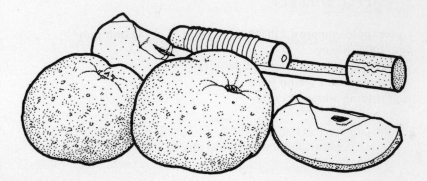

6. Wild Fruit and Savoury Ices

The moment the dew starts to be heavy on the grass in the mornings and the blackberries start to ripen and the elderberries begin to go black and shiny, our local farmer roars up the lane with his mechanical hedge trimmer, and that's that! However, if you don't suffer from this problem, this short section is on ices which you can make from wild fruits gathered from the hedgerows; and very delicious and unusual they are.

ELDERBERRY MOUSSE (Serves 8-10)

This is a fruit with an unusual taste and a marvellous rich colour. Elder bushes vary considerably, some produce sweet berries and others produce bitter ones, full of tannin. If in doubt, be guided by the birds, they will always go for the bush with the sweetest berries.

1 pt (550ml) elderberry *purée* – made from approx. 2 lb (900g) berries
¼ pt (140ml) red grape juice
4 egg yolks
4 oz (100g) raw cane sugar
¼ pt (140ml) water
¾ pt (425ml) cream

Pick enough sprays to make 1 pint *purée*, (approximately 2 lb). Any left over can be used to make elderberry fool or elderberry wine.

Strip the berries from the stalks with a fork and stew gently with a couple of tablespoonsful of red grape juice until soft. *Purée* and sieve. Taste, and add sugar and lemon juice, if required.

Make up the ice cream as for iced Damson Mousse, and fold in the elderberry *purée* just before you fold in the whipped cream.

ROSE HIP WATER ICE

This is not only delicious, but also a rich source of vitamin C.

Rose hips are a very tedious and prickly fruit to pick, and you will need 2 lb for this ice, but with the appropriate bribes it might be a way of occupying children on a fine afternoon in September or October. Even the commercial makes of rose hip syrup are largely dependent for their raw material on children gathering wild rose hips from the hedgerows.

2 lb (900g) rose hips
1 pt (550ml) water
½ lb (225g) honey
juice of 1 lemon
½ teaspoonful agar agar

Boil the rose hips with the water in a lidded saucepan for five to ten minutes, and when they are cool mash them with your hands or in a bucket with a piece of hardwood. Strain the mixture, then return the juice to the saucepan with the honey and the lemon juice and bring to the boil, stirring to dissolve the honey. Now sprinkle the agar agar on to the boiling liquid and stir briskly to dissolve. Cool, chill and freeze.

Variation: Add 2½ fl oz mead (home-made or bought) just before you freeze the ice.

ROSE HIP WATER ICE 2. Instead of going out and picking the berries, buy a packet of rose hip tea, make a strong infusion with 1 pint water and proceed as for the above recipe.

SLOE GRANITA WITH SLIVERED ALMONDS

2 lb (900g) sloes
¾ pt (425 ml) water
6 oz (175g) raw cane sugar
½ teaspoonful agar agar
1 teaspoonful chopped blanched almonds
2-3 tablespoonsful sloe gin

Sloes, which ripen between September and November, are laborious to pick, but well worth the trouble. If we have any left over from our sloe gin, we use them to make this unusual granita.

Simmer the sloes in ½ pint water until the juice is extracted (about twenty minutes), mashing from time to time to help the process. Boil together the sugar and ¼ pint water for five minutes. Strain the sloe juice into the syrup, bring up to the boil, sprinkle on the agar agar and stir briskly to dissolve. Add the sloe gin. Chill and freeze according to directions for granitas.

SAVOURY ICES

An ice does not always have to come at the end of a meal. In Victorian times, when a formal dinner was a long drawn-out affair with six or seven rich courses, or more, these were often interspersed with sorbets to cleanse the palate and no doubt to give the bloated diner a slight breather. Those days are long gone, but a savoury ice can be an attractive and original starter on a hot summers day. It is light and refreshing, and it has the added advantage that you can prepare it well in advance.

Many recipes for iced soups will adapt to become sorbets. Try serving two contrasting sorbets in a glass dish – tomato with cucumber, or beetroot with Stilton ice.

Unless otherwise stated, quantities are for six to eight people.

AVOCADO SORBET WITH PECANS (Serves 4)

3 ripe avocados
4 fl oz (100ml) sour cream
1 tablespoonful lemon juice
Tabasco sauce, sea salt and black pepper
1 egg white, whipped
½ oz (15g) chopped pecans

If you live in a country where avocados are always plentiful, or you pick the right moment when they are cheap in England, this makes a delicious starter. Remember that the seasoning must be strong, or you will end up with an ice that looks an attractive pale green, but tastes bland and dull.

Sieve or liquidize the avocados with the lemon juice. Fold in the sour cream. Season with Tabasco, sea salt and black pepper. Chill and freeze until mushy, then beat and fold in the whipped egg white. Lastly, fold in the chopped pecans. Pack and freeze.

BEETROOT SORBET

This has a marvellous colour and a delicate taste. Serve on its own, or with a cucumber sorbet or a Stilton ice.

1½ lb (675g) beetroots
1 pt (550ml) water
lemon juice to taste
½ a 4 fl oz (100ml) carton of yogurt or sour cream
½ teaspoonful agar agar
sea salt and black pepper

Peel the beetroot and grate coarsely. Simmer gently in the water for half an hour or until tender, then cool and liquidize. Add the lemon juice and season to taste.

Pour back into the saucepan, add the agar agar and bring to the boil. Stir to dissolve the agar agar. Cool, test the seasoning, then freeze to a mush.

Liquidize quickly with the yogurt or sour cream. Pack quickly into the container in which you will store it, and freeze.

CRANBERRY WATER ICE WITH PORT

This makes an attractive starter, and is also delicious with cold meat.

1½ lb (675g) cranberries
½ pt (275ml) apple juice
2oz (50g) raw cane sugar
2½ floz (70ml) port
½ teaspoonful agar agar

Simmer the cranberries with ¼ pint of the apple juice for thirty minutes to extract the juice. Strain, and make up to 1 pint with the remaining apple juice. Return to the saucepan, add the sugar, bring to the boil, stirring to dissolve the sugar. Add the port. When boiling, add the agar agar and whisk to dissolve. Chill and freeze.

When half frozen, remove the ice mixture from the freezer and beat until smooth, or liquidize. Pack and freeze.

Variations:
1. This is a recipe which is equally good with other berries. Try bilberries, whinberries or blackcurrants, with or without the port.
2. Instead of sugar, use 2 tablespoonsful apple jelly.
3. Instead of port, try blackcurrant or elderberry wine.

CUCUMBER SORBET (Serves 4)

This makes a pretty and refreshing start to a summer meal. Serve it in a glass dish with a sorbet of contrasting colour – beetroot, for instance. Garnish with chopped mint or watercress.

1 large cucumber – should give you just over 1pt (550ml) purée
1 green pepper
juice of 1 lemon
1 4floz (100ml) carton of yogurt
1 egg white
1 teaspoonful sea salt and black pepper

Peel the cucumber and cut it into chunks. Cut the pepper into four and remove the seeds. Liquidize the cucumber and green pepper, with salt,

Wonder Bites

6 oz.   Icing Sugar
3 oz.   Margarine
2 oz.   cherries   (chopped)
2 oz.   Walnuts   (chopped)
3-4 oz. coconut
1 Yeasp. Camp Coffee
½ Block K.B. Choc.

Cream marg. & sugar. Add coffee,

walnuts. Roll into small balls, and leave to set in fridge. Coat with melted chocolate and decorate with piece of walnut.

to a pulp. Add yogurt and lemon juice to taste. Turn out into a suitable container for freezing and adjust the seasoning. Freeze to a mush, then put the mixture back into the liquidizer with one beaten egg white.

Liquidize quickly, and pack immediately into the containers in which you wish to store it and return to the freezer.

Variations: In this recipe, the green pepper gives a little bite to the mixture and deepens the colour. You could also try the following:
1. Liquidize the cucumber with six spring onions instead of the pepper.
2. Add an infusion of fresh mint to the cucumber when you liquidize it. For the infusion, take a handful of mint leaves picked from the stalks. Pour over ¼ pint boiling water. Leave covered for half an hour. Strain and use. To serve: decorate with fresh mint leaves.

ICED CURRY SHERBET

1 tablespoonful vegetable oil
1 tablespoonful curry powder (preferably garam masala, which is mild, or your own blend)
1 medium onion, chopped
1 stalk celery, chopped
1 pt (550ml) strong vegetable stock
1 bay leaf
lemon juice, sea salt and black pepper
1 teaspoonful sugar
1-2 tablespoonsful apricot purée or raw sugar jam
2-3 tablespoonsful cream, lightly whipped
½ teaspoonful agar agar

Soften the onion and the celery in the oil over a low heat for ten minutes with the curry powder. Add the vegetable stock, bay leaf, lemon juice and seasonings and simmer for thirty minutes. Remove the bay leaf, *purée* the mixture and return it to the saucepan. Add the apricot *purée* or jam and stir until dissolved. Adjust the seasoning.

Bring to the boil, add the agar agar and stir until dissolved. Cool and freeze to a mush. Beat in the cream, pack quickly and freeze.

To serve, garnish with watercress or chopped parsley, and top with a twist of lemon or a sprinkling of slivered toasted almonds.

LIME SORBET (See page 59)

Try this as a starter. At the final beating, fold in toasted flaked chopped almonds, and garnish with thin slices of cucumber and green peppers.

MINT SORBET

If you were living in the nineteenth century, when a dinner consisted of five or six courses or more, this sorbet would have been ideal to cleanse the palate between courses. As you are a hundred years too late, serve it as a delicious light starter.

**1 quart mint leaves, picked from the stalk and infused with
1 pt (550ml) water
5 oz (150g) apple or crab apple jelly
juice of 1 lemon
a few drops of green colouring – optional
½ teaspoonful agar agar
1 egg white**

This is a really light refreshing start to a summer meal.

To make the infusion, pour the boiling water over the mint leaves, and leave covered for at least half an hour. (When cool, I always squeeze the leaves by hand to extract the last drops of juice.)

Strain and return to the pan with the apple jelly. Bring to the boil, stirring to dissolve the jelly. When boiling, sprinkle on the agar agar and stir to dissolve. Add the lemon juice to taste and colouring if liked. Cool and freeze to a mush. Beat until smooth, or liquidize. Add the egg white, then pack quickly and freeze.

To serve: Garnish with a sprig of fresh mint. If it is the right time of year and your mint is in flower, this looks pretty as a garnish. Avoid chopped mint as this goes black so quickly.

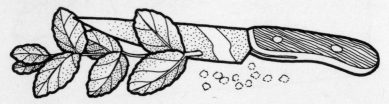

STILTON ICE

You can use any blue cheese for this, which is a rather more solid starter than the others in this section. Adjust the seasoning according to the saltiness of your cheese.

5 oz (150g) grated blue cheese
3 oz (75g) cream cheese
3 spring onions, finely chopped and simmered in ¼ pt milk
sea salt, black pepper, lemon juice or Tabasco
½ pt (275ml) sour cream
1 egg white

Beat together or liquidize all the ingredients except the egg white. Chill and freeze to a mush. Beat into the stiffly whisked egg white. Pack and return to the freezer. Serve topped with a radish flower or radish slices for colour and crunch.

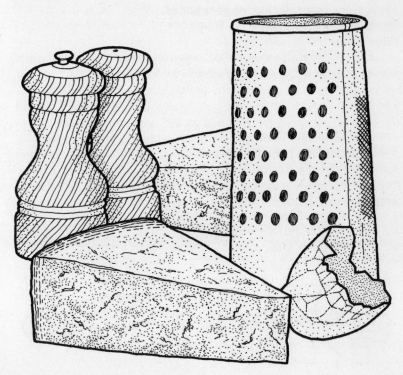

TOMATO SORBET (1)

This is a delicious recipe which works very well with tinned tomato juice, but ideally if you have time it is best made with fresh tomatoes skinned and pulped.

1pt (550ml) tomato juice or 1½ lb (675g) fresh tomatoes, skinned, liquidized and sieved to remove pips
2 spring onions, finely chopped
1 teaspoonful celery seed
1 dessertspoonful Holbrook's Worcester sauce or lemon juice
1 egg white
3 tablespoonsful yogurt
sea salt and black pepper
fresh chives or basil to garnish

Liquidize the tomato juice, spring onions, celery seeds, Holbrook's Worcester sauce, yogurt and seasonings. Adjust the seasoning and freeze to a mush. Liquidize with one egg white stiffly whisked, pack quickly and freeze.

Serve topped with a spoonful of yogurt and a sprinkling of chopped chives or, best if you can get it, fresh basil.

Variation:

1pt (550ml) tomato juice
1 dessertspoonful cider vinegar
1 teaspoonful raw cane sugar
sea salt and black pepper
1 egg white
2 spring onions, finely chopped
½ green pepper, finely chopped
¼ cucumber, finely chopped

Sprinkle the chopped cucumber with a little salt and set aside. Mix the tomato juice with the cider vinegar, salt and pepper. Freeze to a mush. Whisk in the egg white. Rinse and drain the cucumber.

At the last minute, before you pack and freeze, fold in the finely chopped vegetables.

Note: If the vegetables are not finely chopped, they will be tough and rubbery when frozen.

TOMATO SORBET (2)

In this recipe the tomatoes are cooked.

1½ lb (675g) tomatoes, chopped
2 or 3 shallots, chopped, or 6 spring onions
¼ pt (140ml) water
juice of 1 lemon
a good sprig of mint
sea salt and freshly milled black pepper
1 egg white

Simmer all the ingredients except the lemon juice and egg white together to a pulp. Sieve, add the lemon juice and adjust the seasoning. Chill, then freeze to a mush. Add the whipped egg white. Pack and freeze.

To serve: Allow one large tomato for each person, scoop out the flesh. Turn the tomato shells upside down to drain for five minutes. Place a scoop of tomato sorbet in each shell, and top with a sprig of fresh mint.

7. Iced Treats for Children

Few children can resist the temptation of a gaudy multi-coloured ice cream mixed with fruit or nuts or both, and topped with a sauce and a dollop of whipped cream. Here are a few suggestions for such delights. If you have a selection of several ice creams in your freezer, the obvious favourites being chocolate, raspberry, and indeed most of the highly coloured ones, these are very little trouble to produce.

There are also suggestions for a Yule log to replace the Christmas pudding which a lot of children find too rich, and two birthday cakes which will certainly be given no opportunity to sit around melting.

In a less extravagant vein I have included several suggestions for iced lollies. In place of the synthetic highly-coloured tooth-rotters you can buy in the shops, why not give the children an ice which is not oversweet, and is a refreshing natural source of vitamin C? For these it is worth investing in a few iced lolly moulds, available in freezer shops, rather than improvizing. You then have a treat which is quick to make and easy to store and serve. After all, an iced lolly is simply a frozen flavoured syrup – no stirring or hovering about waiting until it is ready to beat. Just mix the syrup, pour into the mould and freeze.

Finally, I have included a few milk lollies. Other recipes for milk ices which children will enjoy are to be found in the section on alternatives to cream.

APRICOT AND ALMANDINE SUNDAE

Place a scoop of apricot ice cream and a scoop of almandine ice cream in a tall sundae glass. Top with orange sauce and whipped cream and surround with stewed apricots.

CHOCOLATE AND PRALINE SUNDAE

Place a scoop of chocolate ice cream and a scoop of praline ice cream in a tall glass. Top with hot chocolate sauce and whipped cream (see Sauces).

FUDGE SUNDAE

Place a scoop of fudge ice cream and a scoop of cherry ice cream in a tall glass. Top with fudge sauce and chopped cashew nuts.

STRAWBERRY SUNDAE

Top strawberry and vanilla ice creams with redcurrant sauce, whipped cream and fresh strawberries.

BANANA SPLIT

For each person:
1 banana
1 scoop each of 3 different ice creams
2½ fl oz (70ml) whipped cream
chopped nuts or fruit to garnish

Slit the banana lengthwise. Put the scoops of ice creams between the two halves. Pipe a fat ribbon of whipped cream along the top and garnish with fruit or chopped hazelnuts. Serve in individual dishes.

Suggested combinations:
Banana, carob and coffee ice creams topped with toasted sesame seeds.

Toffee, hazelnut and apple ice creams topped with grated carob.

Brown bread, loganberry and gooseberry ice creams topped with fresh raspberries.

KNICKERBOCKER GLORY

8 fl oz (225ml) raspberry ice cream
8 fl oz (225ml) banana ice cream
4 peaches
½ lb (225g) raspberries
¼ pt (140ml) whipped cream
toasted sunflower seeds to garnish

Take four tall sundae glasses. (Tall lager glasses will do equally well.) Peel and slice the peaches. Whip the cream. Divide the raspberries between the four glasses. Next, put in a scoop of banana ice cream. Follow this with a layer of sliced peaches, top with a scoop of raspberry ice cream. Finish with a good dollop of whipped cream, or pipe it in an elegant rosette. Sprinkle with sunflower seeds and serve.

You can use any combination of fruits and ice cream you like for this, depending on what you have in the freezer and what is in season at the time. Bananas with chocolate and coffee ice creams are a great favourite in our family, but remember when you slice the banana to sprinkle it with lemon juice to stop it discolouring.

CHILDREN'S BIRTHDAY CAKE (1)
(Serves 14-16)

2 pt (1l 100ml) chocolate ice cream
2 pt (1l 100ml) vanilla ice cream
butter cream icing
whipped cream sweetened with light muscovado sugar to decorate

Soften your ice creams until they can be worked easily (approximately 45 minutes at room temperature, depending on the weather and the time of year). Pack them in alternate layers into a square two-litre polythene container or metal cake tin. Freeze until firm (two to three hours).

Make your butter icing, flavoured with coffee or vanilla. Whip the cream and sweeten to taste. Have both ready in piping bags, because you will have to work fast in the decorating stage.

Dip the container in warm water for a few seconds then ease the edges with a knife and turn the ice cream out onto a cake board. Decorate with the whipped cream and icing. Replace in the freezer until needed.

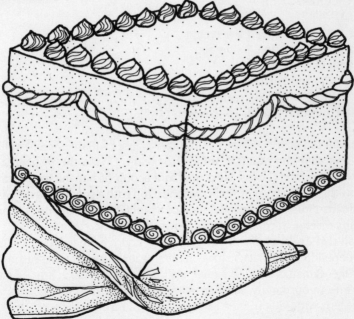

NUMBER BIRTHDAY CAKE (2)

This sort of birthday cake is extravagant in that it will take up to 8 pints of ice cream, but it is worth it for the pleasure it will give.

Have ready a rectangular cake board long enough to take two blocks side by side, of the ice cream of the birthday child's choice, frozen in two-litre square containers. You will also need a palette knife and a jug of hot water to dip it in, a sharp knife, and whipped sweetened cream or whatever you choose to decorate it with.

When the ice cream is just soft enough to cut, turn out the two blocks onto a board. Straighten the two sides which are next to each other, smooth with the hot palette knife and push them together, smoothing over the join with the hot knife.

Now score with your knife on top of the ice cream where you are going to cut, to carve the block into the number corresponding to the child's age. Cut out the shape. Smooth over the surfaces of the carved number with the hot palette knife and replace it in the freezer for a minimum of thirty minutes. (You can re-freeze the ice cream that is left over.)

Take out your number cake, move it onto the cake board, decorate, and replace it in the freezer until needed.

CHRISTMAS LOG

2 pt (1l 100ml) rum and raisin or hazelnut ice cream
1 pt (550ml) carob or chocolate ice cream

First, slightly soften the rum and raisin or hazelnut ice cream. Press it into an oblong loaf tin and return it to the freezer to harden for a few hours. Have ready a palette knife in a jug of hot water.

Soften the carob ice cream until you can spread it. Turn out the rum and raisin ice cream onto a board and cover it with the carob, making it roughly into a log shape with the palette knife. Make a swirl in the ends with a fork and return it to the freezer for an hour.

Make fork marks along it to look like bark and even a knot or two. Transfer it onto a cake board, wrap and return it to the freezer until needed. Decorate with sprigs of holly before serving.

LOVELY LOLLIES

You can make iced lollies with any fruit juice or *purée*. Just sweeten it to taste and pour the liquid into your iced lolly moulds and freeze. Remember that cold numbs the taste buds, so make the flavour strong.

One drawback to the combination of small children and iced lollies is the way the lolly melts and trickles down the arm, covering the child, the furniture and anything else that comes into contact with the sticky mess. If you add agar agar to your syrup – ½-1 teaspoonful per pint – this will help to counteract the problem by making the ice less runny as it melts.

And wrap some kitchen paper round the lolly stick to catch the drips before giving it to the child.

APPLE LOLLY (quick and easy)

To 3 fl oz (80 ml) concentrated apple juice add 12 fl oz (330 ml) water. Pour into the moulds and freeze.

BLACKCURRANT LOLLY

1 pt (550 ml) blackcurrant purée or juice
2 oz (50 g) honey

Dissolve the honey in ¼ pint (140 ml) of the fruit juice or *purée* over a gentle heat. Mix with the rest of the juice, pour into ice lolly moulds and freeze.

ORANGE LOLLY (quick and easy)

1 6 fl oz (165 ml) tin concentrated frozen orange juice

Dilute with ½ pint (275 ml) water, pour into moulds and freeze.

LEMON LOLLY

¼ pt (140ml) lemon juice
¾ pt (425ml) water
1 tablespoonful honey
1 teaspoonful agar agar

Bring the honey, lemon juice and water to the boil. Sprinkle on the agar agar, stir briskly to dissolve. Chill, pour into moulds and freeze.

GOOSEBERRY LOLLY

1 pt (550ml) gooseberry *purée*
1 oz (25g) light muscovado sugar
3 tablespoonsful water

Dissolve the sugar in the water over a low heat. Mix with the gooseberry *purée*. Test for taste, pour into the lolly moulds and freeze.

MELON LOLLY

If you have a really sweet melon, a dessertspoonful of honey will be enough to sweeten it. Scoop out the flesh of the melon, put it in the liquidizer with the honey and a squeeze of lemon juice if liked. Pour into the moulds and freeze.

PEAR LOLLY

For the best taste, peel, core and liquidize 1¼ lb (550g) raw pears with a squeeze of lemon juice. By using this method, the pears are bound to discolour. If you wish to preserve the colour, prepare a light syrup with a tablespoonful of honey and ¼ pint (140ml) water. Drop the pieces of pear into this as you peel them, and simmer them with a good squeeze of lemon juice for five minutes. Sprinkle on 1 teaspoonful agar agar and stir briskly to dissolve.

Cool, liquidize pour into moulds and freeze.

REDCURRANT LOLLY

1 pt (550ml) redcurrant juice
2 tablespoonsful concentrated white grape juice or ¼ pt (140ml)
apple juice

Mix, pour into moulds and freeze.

ROSE HIP LOLLY

You could make this by pounding and boiling fresh rose hips, or,
quicker and easier, make 1 pint (550ml) strong rose hip tea (available in
sachets from most wholefood stores), sweeten with 2 tablespoonsful of
red grape juice or 1 tablespoonful of honey. Add a squeeze of lemon
juice to taste, pour into moulds and freeze.

GRAPE LOLLY (quick and easy)

1 pt (550ml) red grape juice

Pour into moulds and freeze.

TWO-TONE LOLLIES

Half fill the lolly mould with one mixture. Freeze, then top up with
second mixture and return to the freezer.

Good combinations: Blackcurrant and lemon, melon and raspberry,
redcurrant and peach, apple and blackberry.

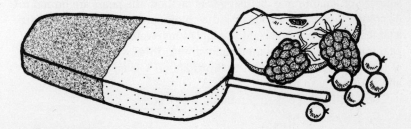

MILK LOLLIES

Some of these can be made in a few minutes by blending in a liquidizer milk and *puréed* fruit, or other flavourings such as honey, malt or coffee.

However, when using fruit with a high acid content such as rhubarb or redcurrant, it is wise first to heat the milk with a little arrowroot to prevent curdling.

BANANA MILK LOLLY

½ pt (275 ml) milk
4 bananas
raw cane sugar to taste

Blend the milk with the bananas and sugar; pour the mixture into lolly moulds and freeze.

MAPLE SYRUP MILK LOLLY

3-4 oz (75-100g) maple syrup
1 pt (550 ml) milk

Dissolve the maple syrup with the milk over a low heat. Pour into lolly moulds and freeze.

Variation: Use malt extract instead of maple syrup.

CAROB LOLLY

6 oz (175g) carob bar
¾ pt (425 ml) milk

Melt the carob bar in milk over a low heat, whisking to mix thoroughly. Pour into lolly moulds and freeze.

Alternatively use 4 oz plain chocolate instead of carob.

PEACH MILK LOLLY

3 medium peaches
1 tablespoonful mild honey
½ pt (275ml) milk

This is best made with fresh peaches. Peel and stone the peaches. Liquidize the fruit with 1 tablespoonful honey and ½ pt milk. Pour into lolly moulds and freeze.

RASPBERRY OR STRAWBERRY MILK LOLLY

2 tablespoonsful clear honey
½ lb (225g) strawberries or raspberries
½ pt (275ml) milk

Dissolve the mild clear honey in the milk over a low heat. Liquidize this with the raspberries or strawberries. Pour into ice lolly moulds and freeze.

BLACKCURRANT MILK LOLLY

½ pt (275ml) milk
1 level teaspoonful arrowroot mixed with 1 tablespoonful cold water
½ lb (225g) fresh blackcurrants, topped and tailed
1 oz (25g) raw muscovado sugar

Dissolve the sugar in the milk over a low heat. Add the arrowroot and bring to the boil, stirring briskly until it thickens. Allow this mixture to cool slightly, combine it with the blackcurrants and liquidize. Pour into the lolly moulds and freeze.

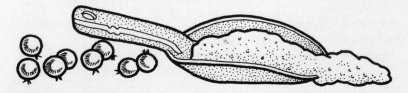

MILK SHAKES

I have included some suggestions for milk shakes – very popular with children, and if you have a liquidizer and your own ice creams in the freezer you can make delicious milk drinks in a matter of seconds.

BANANA MILK SHAKE

Combine in the liquidizer 2 bananas, ½ pint (275ml) milk, and ¼ pint (140ml) vanilla ice cream. Pour into glasses and serve at once.

STRAWBERRY MILK SHAKE

Combine in the liquidizer ½ pint (275ml) milk, ¼ pint (140ml) strawberry ice cream, 6 oz (175g) fresh or frozen strawberries. Pour into glasses and serve at once.

MALT MILK SHAKE

Combine in the liquidizer ½ pint (275ml) milk, ¼ pint (140ml) malt ice cream, ½ oz (15g) cashew nuts, ½ oz (15g) raisins.

8. Special Occasion Desserts

If you have a selection of ices in your freezer you will find that you can produce an impressive creation with surprisingly little trouble. Experiment with your own exciting combinations, it is well worth giving it a try.

Note: The difficulty with serving ice creams at a party is their tendency to melt before you want them to. To prevent this:

1. Always chill your serving dish or bowl.

2. If your ice cream is going to have to stand at room temperature for half an hour or more, arrange it on its serving dish an hour before you need it and return it to the freezer to become firm.

3. Try serving your ice cream in a bowl set in another bowl of crushed ice. I find that if I do this, it stays firm for an hour or more.

Quantities:

Once you know the number of people you have to feed, pick your mould and measure it. A 1 pint mould will be enough for four people. If your bombe is to have three layers, take ½ pint of each ice cream. You can always re-freeze what you don't need, and it is safer to have too much rather than too little.

Bombes

These make the most impressive party ices. The dish is built up, from the outside inwards, of several layers of ice cream. Line the bowl with an ice cream which freezes hard, such as chocolate. The next layer could be a water ice or sorbet, and the middle filled with an iced mousse, but you can have as many or as few layers as you like. It is easier to freeze and unmould if you use a special *bombe* mould, but any metal jelly mould, bowl or cake tin will do.

Basic Method:
Decide on the combination of ices you will use. Take the ice which will form the outside layer from the freezer and soften it for half an hour to an hour, at room temperature. Chill your metal mould and a metal spoon.

Smooth the ice cream up the sides of the mould with the metal spoon, starting from the bottom, until it is completely lined. Return it to the freezer to become firm and take the next ice out to soften. After half an hour to one hour, smooth on the second layer. Finally, repeat the process for the iced mousse, which goes in the centre. Level the top, cover and return to the freezer.

To unmould, half an hour to an hour before serving, remove from the freezer, dip the mould in warm water for a few seconds, dry it, loosen the bombe very gently round the edges and turn it out onto a chilled dish. Decorate it with whipped sweetened cream if you like, and place in the refrigerator for half an hour before you serve it. To serve, slice it with a knife which has been dipped in hot water.

Suggestions:
1. Try different combinations of chocolate ice cream (custard base), iced coffee mousse (adapt the basic recipe for iced mousse with yolks and coffee), and iced praline mousse.
2. Iced almandine mousse, nectarine or peach sorbet and iced raspberry mousse.
3. Spiced plum mousse, damson sorbet and hazelnut mousse.
4. Chocolate, chestnut and vanilla flavours together.

Neapolitans
These are made on the same principal as a *bombe*, except that the ice is frozen in flat layers in a square or oblong mould so that when you turn it out you can see the different layers in contrasting colours and flavours.

Ices in Fruit Cases

These make an attractive dessert. Fruits such as melon, pineapple, grapefruit and orange can be turned into very pretty serving dishes for ice creams or sorbets. The ice can be stored in its fruit case, and needs less last-minute attention than a *bombe* or Neapolitan.

1. *Stuffed Melon*

Slice the top off your melon, scoop out the flesh carefully. Turn the melon shell upside down to drain. Retain the lid.

Make a melon sorbet according to the recipe. When it is ready, return it to the melon case in scoops, replace the lid, wrap and store in the freezer.

Just before serving, remove the lid and top with a spoonful of fresh raspberries. Replace the lid at a jaunty angle.

2. *Stuffed Oranges*

Take one orange for each person. Slice off the top and scoop out the flesh of the orange with a grapefruit knife. Leave the orange upside down to drain and use the flesh to make your sorbet. When the sorbet is frozen, fill the orange case, pressing the sorbet well down with the back of a metal spoon. Replace the lid. Wrap and return to the freezer.

Variation: Follow the same method using grapefruit.

3. *Stuffed Pineapple*

First, lay the pineapple on its side and cut it in half lengthwise. Scoop out the flesh and use it to make a pineapple sherbet. When the sherbet is frozen, return it to the pineapple shell in scoops, wrap up well in cling film and return it to the freezer until needed. It will keep for up to a month.

Variation: Fill the pineapple shell with scoops of different coloured sorbets and sherbets, for example:

1. Pineapple, raspberry and nectarine.
2. Guava, mango and pineapple.
3. Pineapple, orange and strawberry.

9. Alternatives to Cream and Sugar

Ices do not necessarily have to be made with cream. As you may be all too aware, many commercial ice creams have never been within a sniff of it, and contain all sorts of vegetable oil substitutes. There follows a few suggestions for delicious ices made with alternatives to cream.

Bear in mind that it is the fat content in cream which gives ice cream its smooth texture. The alternatives, with a lower fat content, will therefore have a different texture. They will be thinner, and milk ices in particular will tend to be crunchy rather than creamy. You can compensate for this to a certain extent by using arrowroot.

I have included some recipes using yogurt. The sweet, sharp taste this gives is wonderfully refreshing. In other countries, particularly Greece, yogurt is graded according to fat content. If you make your own yogurt, try for a smoother ice cream making the yogurt with half cream and half milk.

There are also recipes using cream cheese and cottage cheese. These you can either make yourself or buy. Home-made *fromage blanc* makes delicious ices. In the larger health food stores you can buy *sprese quartz*, a curd cheese which comes in several different strengths and is also good.

There are also several recipes for milk ices, lighter and more digestible for small children than those with a high fat content. If cow's milk cannot be tolerated, it can be replaced by goat's milk or soya milk, but in this case I find that the most successful ices are the strongly flavoured ones, as both goat and soya milk have a strong flavour of their own, which is better masked.

Finally, there is a recipe for an ice with vegetable oil, for those who cannot tolerate animal fats at all.

APPLE CHEESE ICE CREAM

½ lb (225g) fromage blanc
1 lb (450g) apples
4 tablespoonsful water
juice of ½ lemon
½ oz (15g) butter
4 oz (100g) raw cane sugar
2 egg whites

To make the apple *purée*, peel, core and slice the apples and put them in a saucepan with the butter, sugar, water and lemon juice. Cook very gently until soft. Remove from the heat, mash them to a rough pulp and leave to cool. Beat the apple pulp into the cheese, fold in the stiffly beaten egg whites, pack and freeze.

To serve: Either sprinkle with toasted sunflower seeds or serve with hazelnut meringue (see section on Stores).

*Note:*Ice creams made with cheese need a little extra time to soften before serving, as they freeze very hard.

COTTAGE CHEESE DESSERT

¾ lb (350g) cottage or curd cheese
6 fl oz (165ml) milk
6 oz (175g) honey
3 egg whites
pinch of sea salt

Warm the honey gently in a saucepan until it is runny. Put the cottage cheese, honey and milk in the blender and mix until smooth. Whisk the egg whites with a pinch of salt until stiff, and fold into the mixture. Freeze to a mush, stirring occasionally. Beat until smooth, pack and freeze.

This ice cream has a clean refreshing taste which goes beautifully with fruit, fresh or stewed.

DATE AND PECAN CREAM

1 lb (450g) fromage blanc
juice of 1 lemon
4 oz (100g) mild honey
2 egg whites
pinch of sea salt
3 oz (75g) chopped stoned dates
1 oz (25g) chopped pecan nuts

Warm the honey with the lemon juice to dissolve it, but do not boil. Beat this into the cheese. Whisk the egg whites with the salt and fold them into the mixture. Fold in the chopped dates and pecan nuts. Pack and freeze. To serve, slice rather than scoop.

Variation: Instead of dates and pecans, fold in 3 oz (75g) of stoned sweet cherries which you have previously soaked in a little red grape juice.

GOOSEBERRY CHEESE (Serves 8)

This can be made either with *fromage blanc* (the *petit-suisse* type of cheese) if you can get hold of it, or with cream cheese, or a blend of both. An advantage of this ice is that you can freeze it without beating.

1 ¼ lb (550g) gooseberries
¼ pt (140ml) water
4 oz (100g) fromage blanc or cream cheese
4 oz (100g) light raw cane sugar
4 eggs
pinch of sea salt

Simmer the gooseberries with ¼ pint water and the sugar until soft. Liquidize or put through a sieve. Separate the eggs. Beat the yolks with the cheese until smooth. Add the gooseberry *purée*. Whip the whites of egg and fold them into the mixture. Chill, pack and freeze.

LEMON CHEESE ICE

4 oz (100g) cream cheese
½ lb (225g) cottage cheese
2 eggs
3 oz (75g) honey
2 fl oz (55ml) water
juice of 1 lemon
¼ pt (140ml) whipping cream

Separate the eggs. Beat the yolks until pale and creamy. Heat the honey with the water over a low heat until nearly boiling. Pour over the egg yolks, beating continuously, then beat the cottage cheese and the cream cheese into the egg mixture with a wooden spoon and continue beating until smooth. Add the lemon juice. Whip the cream and fold into the mixture. Whisk the egg whites until stiff and fold this into the mixture. Pack and freeze.

YOGURT AND APRICOT ICE (Serves 8)

4 egg yolks
1 pt (550ml) yogurt (preferably home-made, made with ½ milk, ½ cream)
6 oz (175g) honey
3 oz (75g) dried apricots
6 fl oz (165ml) orange juice
½ oz (15g) toasted flaked almonds

Simmer the dried apricots with the orange juice until tender, and set aside to cool, then sieve or liquidize.

Make up the yogurt and honey ice according to basic method. Fold in the apricot and orange juice *purée*. Chill, then freeze, stirring from time to time. Just before packing, fold in the toasted flaked almonds.

YOGURT AND BLACKCURRANT ICE

2 oz (50g) honey
2 tablespoonsful water
4 oz (100g) blackcurrants
4 egg yolks
1 pt (550ml) yogurt
6 oz (175g) honey

First, prepare the blackcurrants: dissolve the honey in the water over a low heat. Bring to the boil and set aside. Top and tail the blackcurrants and pour the honey syrup over them. Leave to soak.

Make up the ice as for yogurt and honey ice and just before packing strain the honey syrup off the blackcurrants and fold them into the mixture. Freeze.

YOGURT AND HONEY ICE CREAM

4 egg yolks
1 pt (550ml) yogurt
6 oz (175g) honey

Beat the egg whites until pale and frothy. Heat the honey over a low heat to just below boiling point. Pour onto the egg yolks and continue to beat until cool. Whisk in the yogurt, chill and freeze.

You will certainly have your private preferences as to which honey you use. Mexican has a good strong flavour, or if you want a more delicate taste, try clover or acacia.

Note: Honey will always boil up when heated, so be sure to keep an eye on it to stop it boiling over.

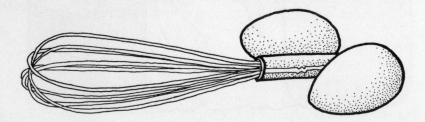

SUGAR ALTERNATIVES

Ices need not necessarily be made with sugar. Black treacle or molasses will make a very strong, rich-tasting ice cream, delicious with spices and dried fruits, though beware of using them with anything delicately flavoured.

Carob syrup and malt extract also make a successful ice cream. Carob syrup gives a strong chocolatey flavour. Malt has a highly individual taste but can go well with other powerful flavours, chocolate for example. It is also good on its own. Maple syrup imparts a mild but subtle flavour.

You can also try out different honeys. The very mild Australian clover is good for many sorbets and sherbets because it does not mask delicate flavours. On the other hand, heather honey gives ice cream a heavier flavour.

I have included a few recipes in this section, as suggestions, but the field is open for you to experiment. As a general rule, these recipes will produce 1½ to 2 pints of ice cream. As they are all fairly rich, this should be enough for six to eight people.

Note: Honey, molasses and other heavy syrups are messy and tiresome to weigh. After a lot of trial and error I think the easiest method is to place the container on the kitchen scales and remove the syrup by the spoonful until the weight of the container is reduced by the amount of syrup needed for the recipe.

HONEY ICE CREAM

The degree of delicacy of the honey used in this recipe determines that of the finished ice cream – the darker the honey, the stronger the flavour.

3 eggs
4 oz (100g) honey
¾ pint (425 ml) whipping cream

Separate the eggs and beat the yolks until thick and foamy, then put them into the top of a double boiler. Heat the honey gently until nearly boiling then pour over the egg yolks and whisk over boiling water until creamy. Remove from the heat and whisk frequently until cold. To speed up chilling, put the bowl or pan over cold water or, even better, ice cubes, before refrigerating. Afterwards, fold in the cream, softly whipped, and finally the egg whites, stiffly whipped with a pinch of sea salt and then freeze.

To serve: Sprinkle with chopped walnuts. If made with a mild honey, a spoonful of honeycomb makes an interesting contrast in texture.

Variations:
1. Fold in 1 lb (450g) apples which have been cooked gently to a *purée* with 2 tablespoonsful of water, ½ oz of butter and 3 tablespoonsful of honey.
2. For spiced apple and honey, mash into the apple *purée* a good pinch of cinnamon and a pinch of nutmeg.
3. Add 2 oz of chopped stem ginger and ¾ teaspoonful of ground ginger. Remember that the flavour of spices fades during the freezing process, so don't be too cautious.

ICED MAPLE SYRUP MOUSSE

3 eggs
4 oz (100g) maple syrup
¾ pint (425 ml) whipping cream

This is a delicately flavoured ice cream.

Separate the eggs and beat the yolks until thick and foamy. Warm the maple syrup over a low heat until nearly boiling, then pour over the egg yolks and whisk over boiling water until creamy. Remove from the heat and whisk frequently until cold. To speed up chilling, put the bowl or pan over cold water or, even better, ice cubes. The more often you whisk, the lighter it will be. Refrigerate.

When cold, fold in the cream, softly whipped. Chill again, then fold in the egg whites, whipped until firm with a pinch of sea salt, then freeze.

To serve: Sprinkle chopped nuts, toasted sesame seeds or sunflower seeds over the top.

Variation: Add ¼ pint strong coffee, either freshly ground or decaffeinated, to the maple syrup and egg yolk mixture. Chopped walnuts are also a good addition.

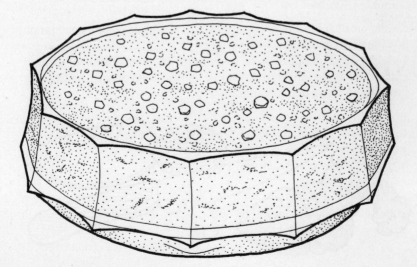

ICED MOUSSE WITH MOLASSES

If you like molasses – and not everybody does – use it instead of sugar to make a very distinctive iced mousse.

3 eggs
1 extra egg white
3 oz (75g) molasses
3 tablespoonsful water
2 oz (50g) chopped dates
1 oz (25g) chopped stem ginger

Separate the eggs and beat the yolks until pale and creamy. Put the egg yolks into the top of a double boiler (or a bowl over a pan of boiling water).

Heat the molasses with the water over a gentle heat until nearly boiling, then pour over the egg yolks and whisk until thick and creamy. Remove from the heat and whisk frequently until cold. To speed up chilling, put the bowl or pan in cold water or, even better, a bowl containing ice cubes. Refrigerate and then whip the cream and fold it in. Whip the egg whites with a good pinch of salt, fold these into the mixture and freeze. As you beat for the last time before packing, stir in the chopped dates and ginger and then freeze.

Variation: Chopped nuts also go well with this mixture. Try ½ oz (15g) chopped walnuts or pecans folded in with the dates and ginger.

ICED LEMON MOUSSE

4 eggs
8 oz (225g) mild honey
6 tablespoonsful lemon juice
grated rind of 1 large lemon
¾ pt (425ml) whipping cream

Separate the eggs. Heat the honey until nearly boiling, then beat the yolks with the honey until thick and creamy. Add the lemon juice and rind. Chill. Whip the cream and fold this into the mixture.

Whisk the egg whites until stiff and fold these into the mixture then chill and freeze.

ICED MOUSSE WITH MALT EXTRACT

4 egg yolks
12 oz (350g) malt extract
¾ pt (425ml) cream

Beat the yolks until thick and creamy. Heat the malt gently until nearly boiling, pour over the egg yolks, beating all the time, and then leave to cool. Whip the cream and fold this into the egg yolk and the malt mixture. Chill and freeze.

RICH DRIED FRUIT ICED MOUSSE

2 oz (50g) raisins
2 oz (50g) dried figs
2 oz (50g) dried apricots
2 oz (50g) dried bananas
½ oz (15g) flaked almonds
½ pt (275ml) orange juice
3 eggs
1 extra egg white
4 oz (100g) carob syrup
¾ pt (425ml) whipping cream

Roughly chop the dried fruits and leave them to soak in the orange juice overnight. Brown the almonds in the oven. This should take no longer than six minutes at 400°F/200°C (Gas Mark 6), but keep an eye on them as they burn easily.

Separate the eggs and beat the yolks until pale and creamy. Heat the carob syrup until nearly boiling and pour it over the egg yolks. Whisk this mixture over hot water (or in a double boiler if you have one) until the mixture is thick like lightly whipped cream, then remove the pan from the heat.

To cool it quickly, put your bowl or the top of your double boiler in a bowl of cold water or, better still, ice cubes. Whisk frequently until cold, then refrigerate.

Whip the cream until it forms soft peaks and fold carefully into the mixture. Then whip the egg whites with a pinch of sea salt until stiff, fold in and freeze. As you beat the mousse for the last time, stir in the drained fruit and the nuts, pack and freeze.

Variation: Try adding 1 tablespoonful of brandy or rum to the orange juice in which the fruit is soaked.

ICED RHUBARB AND GINGER MOUSSE (Serves 8-10)

This looks prettiest if you choose the first rhubarb of the season with a crimson outside skin, so that you end up with a pinkish *purée* rather than a greenish-brown one.

For the purée:
1 lb (450g) rhubarb, chopped
2 oz (50g) preserved stem ginger, very thinly sliced
4 oz (100g) mild honey

6 egg yolks
7 egg whites
¾ pt (425ml) whipping cream
4 oz (100g) mild honey
¼ pt (140ml) water
a good pinch of salt

For the purée: Stew the rhubarb very gently over a low heat, in a lidded saucepan, with the honey and 2 tablespoonsful of water to prevent burning, for fifteen minutes or until tender. Mash to a pulp. Add the sliced ginger and 1 tablespoonful of the syrup from the jar. Set in the refrigerator to chill.

For the mousse: Beat the egg yolks until pale and creamy. Dissolve the honey in the water and bring to the boil. Pour the mixture over the egg yolks, beating all the time. Mix in the rhubarb and ginger *purée*. Whip the cream until thick and then fold it into the mixture. Whisk the eff whites until stiff and then fold in too. Chill and freeze.

Ice Cream for Diabetics
The high calorific value of most ice cream makes it unsuitable for diabetics. If you cut down the sugar content, you will affect the texture of the finished ice cream. However, glycerine can be used in the place of sugar and the mixture will freeze satisfactorily. Artificial sweeteners such as sorbitol could then be used to flavour it.

10. Milk Ices

When, in Victorian times, Italian ice cream vendors started to make an appearance on British streets, the ices they offered were made with milk, sweetened, thickened with cornflour, flavoured and frozen. I prefer arrowroot as a thickening agent, and raw cane sugar as a sweetener, otherwise the method is much the same. You can ring the changes with the sweetener and flavouring of your choice.

As the fat content in these ices is low, the sugar and the arrowroot are important to achieve a smooth texture. Use a little more of both than you would normally.

Basic recipe:

1½ pt (825ml) milk
4oz (100g) raw cane sugar
1 rounded tablespoonful arrowroot – 1oz (25g) scant
flavouring

Mix the arrowroot with 1 tablespoonful of the milk to make a smooth paste. Bring the rest of the milk to the boil with the sugar. Add the arrowroot, stirring briskly to dissolve. Boil for a few seconds to thicken.

Add flavouring. Chill and freeze. Stir with a fork from time to time. When nearly set, beat well, pack and finish freezing.

BANANA MILK ICE

1 pt (550ml) milk
2½ oz (65g) light muscovado sugar
1 rounded dessertspoonful arrowroot
3 bananas

Prepare milk ice as for basic recipe. Very ripe bananas (I use overripe ones) will give the best flavour.

Mash the bananas and fold them quickly into the hot milk mixture. Bananas, once mashed, will discolour quickly if left lying about.

CHOCOLATE MILK ICE

1½ pt (825ml) milk
1 rounded tablespoonful arrowroot − 1 oz (25g) scant
2 oz (50g) raw cane sugar
6 oz (175g) plain chocolate

Thicken the milk and sugar with the arrowroot as for the basic mixture. Place the chocolate in a bowl and pour boiling water over it. When the chocolate is soft, carefully pour off the water, and beat in the hot thickened milk gradually. Return to the saucepan and beat until smooth. Chill and freeze.

Note: This ice cream will freeze fairly hard, so allow enough time for it to soften before serving. If you prefer it softer, add more sugar.

Variation: In place of chocolate, use a 9 oz carob bar.

COCONUT MILK ICE

1½ pt (825 ml) milk
1 rounded dessertspoonful arrowroot
6 oz (175 g) light muscovado sugar
4 oz (100 g) creamed coconut

Heat together the milk, sugar and creamed coconut, stirring to melt the coconut. Thicken with arrowroot, chill and freeze.

Note: Weigh the creamed coconut carefully. If you use too much, the ice will be very hard.

LEMON MILK ICE

1½ pt (825 ml) milk
1 rounded tablespoonful arrowroot – 1 oz (25 g) scant
4 oz (100 g) light muscovado sugar
juice and rind of 1 lemon

Mix the arrowroot with 1 tablespoonful of the milk as for the basic method. Bring the rest of the milk to the boil with the pared rind of lemon and sugar. Thicken with the arrowroot. Allow to cool, then remove the lemon rind. Add the lemon juice and freeze.

PRALINE MILK ICE

1½ pt (825 ml) milk
1 rounded tablespoonful arrowroot – 1 oz (25 g) scant
2½ oz (65 g) praline
2 oz (50 g) light muscovado

Make this ice according to the basic method. Add the praline to the hot thickened milk mixture. Chill and freeze.

Note: You need less sugar in this recipe because of the sugar in the praline.

TOFFEE MILK ICE

4 oz (100g) caramel (see p.114)
1½ pt (825 ml) milk
1 rounded dessertspoonful arrowroot

Follow the basic method, using caramel in place of sugar.

Variation: Use 12 oz (350g) malt extract instead of the caramel.

NON-DAIRY ICE CREAM (Serves 6-7)

6 eggs
6 fl oz (165 ml) vegetable oil
3 oz (75g) light muscovado sugar
flavouring

Separate the eggs. Either beat the egg yolks with the sugar, then add the oil in a steady stream, whisking until thick, or put the egg yolks, sugar and oil in the liquidizer and blend until thick. Add flavouring; e.g. 1 heaped tablespoonful of decaffeinated coffee dissolved in 1 tablespoonful of hot water to a treacly consistency. Whisk the egg whites until stiff and fold into the mixture.

Note: Choose as tasteless an oil as possible (sunflower oil is satisfactory, olive oil is too strong). The flavouring you add must be strong.

Variation:
1. Instead of the decaffeinated coffee, add ¼ pint sweetened damson *purée*.
2. Omit the sugar. Instead, use 3 tablespoonsful caramel (see Stores).

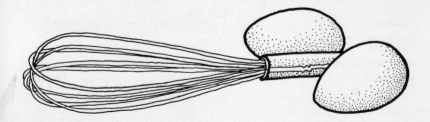

11. Sauces

I have included a few sauces to serve with ice creams. All of them are simple to make and several can be stored in the freezer. Fruit sauces, which are basically fruit *purées* slightly thickened and sweetened, can be made at the same time as you make your fruit *purée* for the ice cream.

Syrups, such as elderflower or maple syrup can be served as a topping for ice creams, as can whipped cream, plain or flavoured.

Try iced prune mousse topped with whipped cream, flavoured with rum.

APRICOT SAUCE

2 oz (50g) dried apricots
1 pt (550ml) orange juice
4 oz (100g) honey
1 rounded teaspoonful arrowroot

Soak the apricots in ¾ pint of the orange juice overnight, then put them in a saucepan with the honey and simmer gently for fifteen minutes until tender. *Purée* the fruit and juice in the liquidizer. Mix the arrowroot with 2 tablespoonsful of orange juice. Return the apricot and orange juice *purée* to the saucepan with the remainder of the orange juice. Bring to the boil and thicken with the arrowroot. Taste and add more orange juice or honey if liked.

Serve hot or cold. This is good with hazelnut, praline or vanilla ices, and can be, stored in the freezer.

BLACKCURRANT SAUCE

½ lb (225g) blackcurrants
¾ pt (425ml) water
4oz (100g) honey
1 rounded teaspoonful arrowroot

Simmer the blackcurrants in ½ pint water and honey for ten to fifteen minutes until tender. *Purée* and sieve the fruit mixture. Mix the arrowroot with 2 tablespoonsful of water. Return the *purée* to the saucepan, add the other ¼ pt (140ml) water, and bring to the boil, thickening with the arrowroot.

Serve hot or cold, with vanilla or brown bread ice. This sauce can also be stored in the freezer.

Note: This fruit sauce is delicious made with other fruits. Try loganberries or cranberries.

BURNT ORANGE SAUCE

See Caramel Sauce – variation.

BUTTERSCOTCH SAUCE

4oz (100g) light muscovado sugar
2 tablespoonsful maple syrup
2oz (50g) butter
½ pt (275ml) whipping cream (or ¼ pt milk, ¼ pt cream)

Put the sugar, syrup and butter over a gentle heat and stir until the sugar has dissolved. Then increase the heat and cook until the sauce turns golden brown, stirring continuously. Remove from the heat and beat in the cream.

Serve this sauce hot or cold. It tastes particularly good with apple, cinnamon and vanilla ices.

CARAMEL SAUCE

4 oz (100g) light muscovado sugar
6-7 fl oz (165-190ml) water
squeeze of lemon juice

Make the caramel as for the toffee ice cream (custard base). Serve hot or cold with praline or vanilla ices. This sauce can be stored in a screw-top jar.

Variation: **BURNT ORANGE SAUCE**
Use orange juice instead of water.

CHESTNUT SAUCE

1 10 oz (275g) tin unsweetened chestnut *purée*
1 lb (450g) light muscovado sugar
½ pt (275ml) water

Dissolve the sugar in the water over a low heat. Bring to the boil and boil fast for three minutes. Cool, and beat the syrup into the chestnut *purée*. Serve with vanilla ice cream.

CHOCOLATE SAUCE

6 oz (175g) plain raw sugar chocolate
1 lb (450g) light muscovado sugar
½ pt (275ml) water

First, make a syrup by dissolving the sugar in the water and boiling this mixture briskly for five minutes. Break up the chocolate and put it in the top of a double boiler. Pour boiling water over it to soften. Pour off the water carefully, then add the hot syrup by degrees, stirring continuously until it is well blended and shiny. Serve hot or cold.

Variations:
1. Instead of chocolate, use a 9 oz carob bar.
2. Add 1 tablespoonful of decaffeinated instant coffee, dissolved in 2 tablespoonsful boiling water, after beating in the syrup.
3. Add rum to taste after beating in the syrup.

ORANGE SAUCE

¾ pt (425ml) orange juice
grated rind of 2 oranges
2 oz (50g) light muscovado sugar
1 rounded teaspoonful arrowroot

Mix the arrowroot with 2 tablespoonsful of orange juice. Bring the rest of the orange juice, sugar and grated orange rind to the boil, stirring to dissolve the sugar. Thicken with the arrowroot and serve hot or cold.

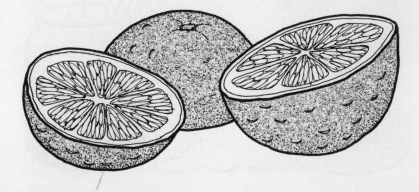

RASPBERRY AND REDCURRANT SAUCE

½ pt (275 ml) redcurrant juice (see Stores Section)
3 oz (75g) honey
6 oz (175g) fresh raspberries
1 rounded teaspoonful arrowroot, mixed in 1 tablespoonful water

Bring the redcurrant juice to the boil with the honey, stirring to dissolve the honey. Thicken with the arrowroot. *Purée* and sieve the raspberries and beat them into the redcurrant sauce. Taste for sweetness. This sauce may be served hot or cold and can also be stored in the freezer.

SPICED PLUM SAUCE

See recipe for Spiced Plum Mousse.

12. Suggested Stores

You can add exciting variety to your ice cream repertoire by keeping a few raw materials to hand in your store cupboard. There follow a few recipes for items such as brown breadcrumbs, toasted hazelnuts, meringues and cookies which will keep for a month or more in an air-tight tin or polythene tub. It also saves time if you have handy such items as toasted seeds – sesame, sunflower or cardamom, for example, and toasted flaked almonds. Added to your ice cream mixture, or sprinkled over the top, they will enable you to ring the changes.

A stock of apple or crab-apple jelly is useful. If you live in the country and are not swamped with boxes and baskets of your own windfalls in the autumn, you will certainly be inundated with offerings from well-meaning neighbours. Turn all these into jelly, and you will have an instant basis for water ices, which you can vary by flavouring with the herb or flower of your own choice, or by adding other fruit juice.

The Freezer
There are also a few stand-bys which are worth keeping in your deep freeze if you have one. The more common fruits such as raspberries or strawberries are usually obtainable from freezer stores during the winter, but it is worth keeping *purées* of such fruits as damsons and elderberries in 1 lb packs. (Remember to label them clearly, if you don't want them to vanish to the bottom of the freezer, to turn up, battered and unidentifiable, a couple of years later.) When you are freezing soft fruits such as loganberries or blackcurrants, bear in mind that if

you want to keep some intact for garnish, it is best to store them in solid tubs rather than polythene bags.

Redcurrants are another fruit not always easy to come by in the winter. Redcurrant juice makes such a difference, both in colour and flavour, to many ices, that it is well worth storing in ½ pint packs. Freeze in square or oblong blocks for ease of storing, then store them in polythene bags.

For infusions, though it is always possible to use dried herbs, I prefer to pick such herbs as mint, lemon balm and tansy in May and June when they are young and tender. Strip the leaves from the stalks and store them in the freezer.

HOME-MADE APPLE JELLY STOCK

This can be stored in sterilized jars and used, either to make jellies from other fruit which lack pectin and therefore do not set easily, or as a stabilizer in sorbets in place of agar agar or arrowroot.

Collect the windfalls and cut up the fruit, removing all the rotten bits, and slice thinly. Weigh and put the apples in a pan with 1 pint of water for each pound of fruit. Simmer for fifteen minutes then strain off the juice through one thickness of cheese cloth or, failing that, a piece of old sheet. Set the juice aside and return the pulp to the pan. Add the same amount of water again, simmer for fifteen minutes, and strain as before.

Combine both lots of juice, bring them to the boil and pour into hot, sterilized bottling jars. Allow to cool, and store.

APPLE OR CRAB-APPLE JELLY

5 lb (2½k) windfall apples or crab-apples
water
honey

Cut up the fruit and remove all the blemished parts. Put the apples in a large pan with just enough water to cover. Simmer until soft then turn into a jelly bag and leave to drip overnight or for eight hours.

Measure the juice and allow 1 lb honey per pint. Put the juice and honey in a large pan and bring slowly to the boil. Boil rapidly until it will set when tested (about twenty minutes).

Note: A large pan is necessary because the honey will boil up.

BROWN BREADCRUMBS

If your family is as addicted to brown bread ice cream as mine is, it is worth making breadcrumbs in quantity and storing them in an air-tight tin, in a cool place.

1 lb (450g) brown breadcrumbs
12 oz (350g) dark muscovado sugar

The easiest way to make brown breadcrumbs is to take the crusts off a wholemeal loaf, and feed the loaf into a liquidizer, a little at a time. Otherwise, you will have to resort to a grater. In a shallow baking tin, thoroughly mix the breadcrumbs and the muscovado sugar with a fork, being careful not to break up the lumps in the sugar. Put this mixture in the oven at 400°F/200°C (Gas Mark 6). Once it starts to brown, it will brown at the edges first, so take it out and stir it with a fork to break it up every five to seven minutes, until it is a rich, even dark brown; this will take half an hour. To test, take a small piece out to cool. If, when it is cool, it is crunchy, your mixture is ready. Turn it out onto a tray to cool.

Now pound it into crumbs with a rolling pin, or put it through the mincer at its coarsest. Store in an air-tight tin.

CARDAMOM COOKIES (to serve with ice cream)

6 oz (175g) butter
8 oz (225g) light muscovado sugar
1 egg, lightly beaten
2 fl oz (55ml) single cream (or top of the milk)
1 lb (450g) wholewheat flour
1 teaspoonful baking powder
2 teaspoonsful ground cardamom

Cream the butter and sugar until fluffy. Add the egg and cream and heat well. In another bowl, sift together the flour, cardamom and baking powder. Add the flour mixture to the butter mixture, beating well until it forms a dough. Knead the dough with your hands until it is smooth.

Roll the dough into two sausage shapes about 2 in. in diameter, wrap in cling film and place in the refrigerator for at least five hours, preferably overnight. Grease a baking sheet and heat the oven to 400°F/200°C (Gas Mark 6). Slice the dough into rings ¼ in. thick.

Bake in the centre of the oven for twelve to fifteen minutes until brown. Cool on a wire rack and then store in an air-tight container.

COCONUT COOKIES

**4 oz (100g) and 1 tablespoonful butter or polyunsaturated
margarine**
3½ oz (90g) light muscovado sugar
3 oz (75g) desiccated coconut
3 oz (75g) rolled oats
6 tablespoonsful cornflakes
1 tablespoonful honey

These are quantities for twice as many cookies as you will need, but
they are well worth having in your store cupboard.

Set the oven to 325°F/170°C (Gas Mark 3). Grease a medium-sized
baking tray with 1 teaspoonful of butter. In a bowl, mix the dry
ingredients. Heat the rest of the butter with the honey in a small
saucepan over a low heat. When it has melted, stir the butter and honey
into the dry ingredients. Drop spoonfuls of the mixture onto the
prepared baking tray and bake in the oven for thirty minutes until
golden brown.

Cool the cookies on a wire rack and store them in an air-tight tin.

ELDERFLOWER SYRUP

4 lb (1 k 800g) gooseberries
3 lb (1 k 350g) light muscovado sugar
1 pt (550ml) water
12 heads of elderflowers

Dissolve the sugar in water over a low heat. Add the gooseberries and simmer gently for ten minutes. Add the heads of elderflowers, remove from the heat and allow to infuse for thirty minutes. Line a nylon sieve with a piece of muslin and strain the juice through this. Return the juice to the saucepan, bring to the boil and pour immediately into hot, sterilized bottling jars.

FUDGE

This is something that is worth making in larger quantities than you need for one recipe and storing it in an air-tight tin – if you can keep your family from picking at it, that is. This recipe will make approximately 2 lb of a slightly crunchy fudge which will contrast well with the smooth texture of ice cream.

4 oz (100g) butter or polyunsaturated margarine
½ pt (275 ml) milk
2 lb (900g) raw cane sugar

Put the butter, milk and sugar into a fairly large saucepan (4-6 pints) and bring it slowly to the boil. You will need a large saucepan because the fudge will boil up. Let it boil furiously for ten minutes or until your sugar thermometer registers 240-250°F/130°C. Do not stir more than you have to to keep it from burning. Now take it off the heat and leave it for two minutes, no longer, or you will have trouble pouring it. Scrape the crystallized fudge off the sides of the saucepan. Beat quickly and pour the mixture into an oiled tin so that it is ¼ in. thick. As it cools, score it with a knife. When it is cold, chop it coarsely or cut it into squares.

HAZELNUT AND LIGHT MUSCOVADO MIXTURE

1 lb (450g) hazelnuts
1 lb (450g) light muscovado sugar

For this you need ground roasted hazelnuts. You can either buy your hazelnuts ready ground, in which case you only have to roast them, or grind and roast your own whole hazelnuts. To do this, place 1 lb of whole hazelnuts in a baking tin in the oven at 400°F/200°C (Gas Mark 6) for about half an hour until they are a rich brown; (remove the tin from the oven and shake the nuts from time to time so that they brown evenly). Now remove the skins, either by rubbing in a clean tea-towel or by rubbing in a sieve.

Grind the hazelnuts in an electric grinder a little at a time. Mix with the brown sugar and store in an air-tight tin. The disadvantage of grinding your own is that you will tend to get a rather solid paste, whereas ready ground hazelnuts remain friable and easy to mix.

To roast ready ground hazelnuts, place them in the oven at 400°F/200°C (Gas Mark 6) in a shallow baking tray for about thirty minutes, stirring often with a fork so that they brown evenly. When brown, remove, mix with the light muscovado sugar and store in an air-tight tin.

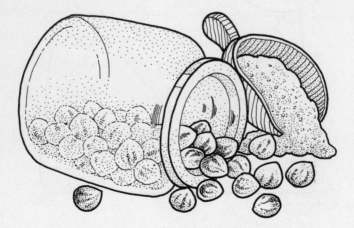

HAZELNUT MERINGUE

6 egg whites
12 oz (350g) light muscovado sugar
1 teaspoonful vinegar
7 oz (200g) ground hazelnuts
pinch of sea salt

Beat out the lumps in the sugar with a rolling pin, and sieve. Whip the egg whites with a pinch of salt. Fold in half of the sugar and continue to whisk until shiny. Add the vinegar, and the remaining sugar and whisk until the mixture stands up in peaks. Fold in the ground hazelnuts.

Spoon the mixture onto an oiled baking sheet, ideally on a sheet of greaseproof paper, and place in the oven at 250°F/130°C (Gas Mark ½) for 2½ hours or until dried out in the middle. Test one by lifting it out and pressing the bottom. Cool on a wire plate rack and then store in an air-tight tin.

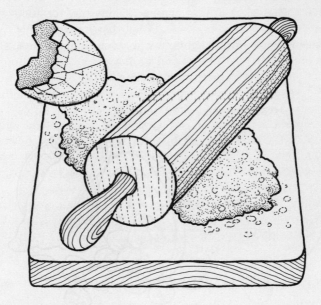

MERINGUES

6 egg whites
12 oz (350g) light muscovado sugar
pinch of sea salt

These store well in an air-tight tin. Set the oven at 225°F/110°C (Gas Mark ¼). Beat out the lumps in the sugar with a rolling pin, and sieve. Whisk the egg whites until firm, then beat in half the sugar and continue whisking until the meringue stands up in peaks. Fold in the remaining sugar. Arrange in spoonfuls on a lightly oiled baking sheet and place in the oven for two hours, or until dried out.

PRALINE

1 lb (450g) almonds (unblanched)
1 lb (450g) raw cane sugar
4 fl oz (110ml) water

Once you know that you like this, it is worth making more than you need for one batch of ice cream, and storing it in an air-tight jar. This recipe will make approximately 2 lb praline.

Put the almonds, water and sugar over a low heat and leave until the sugar melts, keeping an eye on it. When the sugar bubbles and darkens, stir with a metal spoon and continue cooking until the mixture is a good dark brown, but not black! This will take about twenty minutes. As soon as the mixture begins to smoke and the almonds start to pop, take it from the heat. Pour quickly onto an oiled slab or baking sheet and leave it until it has set hard.

Now either pound it to a paste with a pestle and mortar or crush it until it is in crisp, coarse crumbs. Sift it to remove the larger pieces and store it. The texture is a matter of personal taste.

TOASTED FLAKED ALMONDS

These store well in an air-tight tin. To toast, set the oven at 400°F/200°C (Gas Mark 6), place flaked almonds on a baking sheet in the centre of the oven and leave for no more than seven minutes. They burn very easily.

Index